THE
BOOK
OF
LUCK

A Guide to Success, Fortune,
Palmistry and Astrology

Whitman Publishing Company

DOVER PUBLICATIONS, INC.
Mineola, New York

Bibliographical Note

This Dover edition, first published in 2016, is an unabridged
republication of *Everybody's Book of Luck*, originally published
by the Whitman Publishing Co., Racine, Wisconsin,
and Poughkeepsie, New York, in 1900.

International Standard Book Number

ISBN-13: 978-0-486-80890-1
ISBN-10: 0-486-80890-4

Manufactured in the United States by RR Donnelley
80890401   2016
www.doverpublications.com

CONTENTS

CONTENTS

THE
BOOK
OF
LUCK

A Guide to Success, Fortune,
Palmistry and Astrology

THINGS THAT BRING YOU GOOD LUCK
AND BAD LUCK

ASK A dozen people whether they have any superstitions, and the majority will tell you, without hesitation, that they have not the slightest belief in such things. If the truth is told there are very few of us who do not cherish some little weaknesses in this direction. One person may believe in a number of superstitions; another has, perhaps, only a few that are observed; but he or she that has none at all is a remarkably rare individual.

As a matter of fact, most superstitions are based on reason and sound common sense, and the man or woman who pays heed to them is acting intelligently, whether he or she knows it or not. Take, for instance, the belief that it is unlucky to walk under a ladder. True, the old assertion is that it is unlucky to do so because Jesus Christ was taken down from the Cross by means of a ladder. But the more practical reason is that painters and other men on ladders are very likely to drop things and, if you happen to be passing at the time, the paintpot or the tools will fall on you.

Of course, the reasons for all superstitions are not so evident as this one about walking under a ladder: nevertheless, there is a germ of reason in them all, whether or not we know the reason. Thus, the man or woman who observes the common superstitions of everyday life is acting wisely. Not only will he or she avoid a good deal of trouble, but his actions will provide him with a sense of well-being, and the effect it will have on his mind, the psychological effect as it is called, is all to the good.

It is not proposed to explain why this or that superstition is worthy of being observed; in many cases, the reason is obscure; but here we will give some of the beliefs which are current at the present time.

First of all, you should never pass anybody on the stairs of a private house, and, while talking of stairs, it may be said that many people believe that, for someone to fall up a step, is a sign of an approaching wedding.

Never light three cigarettes with the same match unless you are prepared for a spell of ill-fortune. This superstition gained currency during the War, probably because a match held long enough to light three cigarettes would give the enemy a clue to your position, especially at night-time.

If the cord of a picture frame snaps and the picture falls to the ground, it is an omen that somebody is going to die. If the picture is a portrait of a living person, then that person's life is the one likely to be terminated. This omen may be considered a remarkably silly one, with not a shred of sense to recommend it. Yet how many people can point to instances when the prophecy has come true! Of salt, there are several omens. The chief one tells you not to help anybody to salt; in other words, it is unwise to put some on a person's plate. Helping them to salt is helping them to sorrow. Another superstition says

3

that if you spill salt you will be unlucky unless you throw a pinch of it over your left shoulder.

To break a mirror is known by all as a serious matter. The reason why it is unlucky, we are told, doubtless finds its origin in a mere association of ideas. The mirror being broken, the image of the person looking into it is destroyed: therefore, bad luck in some form must be the fate of the careless one. What exactly is the penalty one must pay for breaking a mirror is not definite. Some people speak of seven years of misfortune, while others claim that it means seven years of celibacy.

To take certain things into the house is the height of folly, if you believe in superstitions. May or hawthorn blossom is one, though the berries of this flower seem to have no ill-potency. Peacock's feathers are another. Somewhat similar is the contention that it is very unlucky to open an umbrella indoors.

While sitting at the meal-table, there are several things that must not be done. Helping a friend to salt has been already mentioned, but you must not allow the knives or forks to become crossed. Quarrels with your friends will result if you do. Of course, you must not sit down, thirteen of you, around the table. As is well known, this belief has its origin in the Last Supper, when our Lord sat at meat with his twelve apostles. On the other hand, should you taste a fruit for the first time in that season, you have only to frame a wish and it will be granted. Much the same applies to mince-pies. You will be awarded with a whole happy month for each pie that you eat at Christmas-time which is made in a different house. Of course, it is highly unwise for two people to pour tea out of the same pot at the same meal.

To give a friend an edged tool is sure to cut the friendship, whether it be a knife, a pair of scissors, a razor or a chisel. When such a gift is to be made, the usual plan is to sell it to your friend for a penny.

You should never put a shoe on a table, and, to see a pin lying on the floor and leave it there, is an omen that you will want before you die. As the jingle runs:

> See a pin and let it lie, you're sure to want before you die.
> See a pin and pick it up, then you're sure to have good luck.

Elsewhere, a good deal is said about dreams. Here it will be sufficient to mention one or two items of interest. It is decidedly unlucky to dream of a baby, yet to dream of a funeral is lucky. The following is worth bearing in mind:

> Friday dream and Saturday told;
> Sure to come true, if ever so old.

And here it will be appropriate to recall the fact that it is an unwise thing to get out of bed on the wrong side. The devil will be with you all the day, if you do.

You should avoid looking at the new moon through glass; but if you have a wish that you want fulfilled, you have only to count seven stars on seven nights in succession. Let it be said, however, that to count seven stars for this space of time is not as simple as it appears.

It is unlucky to treasure locks of people's hair, and, should you drop a glove, it is to your advantage if someone else picks it up for you. If the fire refuses to light properly in the morning, anticipate a whole day with the devil.

Everybody knows that one of the luckiest things that can be done is to pick up a horse-shoe. But it is not generally known that the more nails left in it, the better. Nor is it sufficiently well recognized that a shoe, hung up, should have the tips pointing upwards. If they are turned down, the luck will run out of them.

Naturally, you will never start anything fresh on a Friday, and you will not cut your fingernails on a Sunday. Regarding fingernails, a poet, of sorts, has said:

> Cut them on Monday, you cut them for news.
> Cut them on Tuesday, a new pair of shoes.
> Cut them on Wednesday, you cut them for health.
> Cut them on Thursday, you cut them for wealth.
> Cut them on Friday, a sweetheart you'll know.
> Cut them on Saturday, a journey you'll go.
> Cut them on Sunday, you cut them for evil:
> For all the next week, you'll be ruled by the devil.

Of course, bad luck has not a monopoly on your superstitions, for good luck has something to say also. To see a piebald horse is fortunate; to find white heather, four-leaved clover or four-leaved shamrock is even more fortunate. To open a pea-pod and find ten peas in it is particularly lucky. For a black cat to come into your house is worth much. To come across a nickel with a hole in it is not without its merits, but the best thing of all is to put on some article of clothing inside out, and to wear it all day long, without being aware of it until bed-time.

HAVE YOU A TALISMAN?

"A person who finds a four-leaved clover, and believes it is a harbinger of something good, has adopted the right attitude, for he keeps a keen look-out for that particular good and holds out both hands for it. Seldom is he disappointed, for he has unconsciously set going the mental machinery which brings his wishes within reach. Had he not found the clover and had gone along life's highway unexpectant of anything good, he would never have discovered this pleasant happening. And therein lies the true psychology of luck, which seems too simple to be true, but then its simplicity is really the sign-manual of its verity."

This quotation from the writings of a well-known author goes direct to the point about talismans. If you adopt a talisman and put your faith in it, you immediately prepare your mind for receiving an abundance of good fortune. Reject all talismans and argue that there is no such thing as luck, and you straightway set going the mental machinery which looks on the dark side of things and which misses every slice of luck that comes along. Therefore, we say, with emphasis, take to yourself a talisman, a mascot, a charm—call it what you will—and you will never regret it.

Of talismans, there are countless varieties; some are known the world over, others are the particular choice of individuals. They range from the

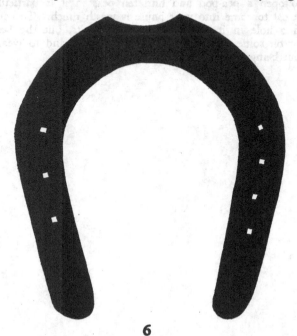

amulets and scarabs of the ancients to the golliwogs and crudities of the ultra-moderns. Your choice may roam between these two extremes, but whatever your choice, it must be set with the seal of your faith.

In order to assist you in picking out a talisman for yourself, we append the following accounts of those examples which are favored most:—

THE HORSE-SHOE.—No symbol is a greater favorite than the horse-shoe. There are many legends regarding its origin, but the most commonly accepted concerns the well-known visit of his Satanic Majesty to the shoe-smith. As a consequence, the Devil evinced a wholesome dread of horse-shoes, and would not go near a house or person possessing one. It is more likely, however, that the horse-shoe was accepted as a symbol of luck because it was a commonplace object very nearly the same shape as the metal crescents worn by the Romans when they wanted to be fortunate. These crescents were always carried with the horns turned up, and, if a horse-shoe is to bring good luck, it, too, must be placed with the prongs uppermost. The reason for the prongs being so turned depends on a belief that misfortune always travels in circles, but when it reaches the tips of a horse-shoe, it is baffled, unless all the luck has already run out of the tips through them being turned downwards.

Of course, an old, worn shoe is more lucky than a new one, and it is a recognized fact that the more nails found in it the luckier will be the finder.

THE SCARAB.—This device is accounted very lucky or very unlucky, according to the disposition of the wearer. The symbol represents the

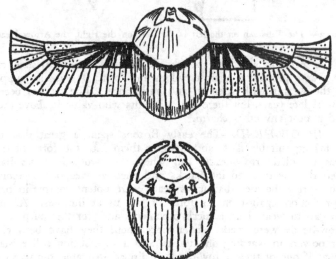

No. 2.—An Egyptian Scarab, such as were used as talismen. Two forms are shown, one with the pectoral wings outspread; the other, with wings closed.

scarab beetle with its wings outspread or with them closed. Such charms are made to-day in large numbers for sale in Egypt, but those who trade in them usually claim that each particular specimen has been in the family since Biblical times. As a rule, the device is made in a rough kind of bluish porcelain and is carved, in intaglio, with divine figures. The Egyptians used to make up the scarab as a neck pendant or as a little ornament for placing in the coffins of the dead. Its mission was to scare away the evil one.

THE TET.—This symbol was shaped somewhat like a mallet, and was always worn with the head uppermost and the handle hanging down. It was made in porcelain or stone, and was often colored gaudily. The Egyptians were the first to find efficacy in this charm, and they wore it suspended

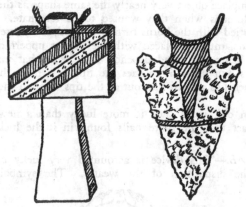

No. 3.—The Talisman on the left is the Tet: on the right, the Arrow Head.

around the neck to ward off attacks from visible and invisible enemies. Thus, it was a protection against evil in any form; it was also supposed to provide the wearer with strength and endurance. The tet has been much forgotten of late years, but there are adherents who value it above the horse-shoe and almost any other charm.

THE ARROW-HEAD.—The early Britons spent a great deal of their time in taking suitable flints and shaping them into the form of triangles. These were called arrow-heads, and when the two side edges had been sharpened they were fixed into sticks and used as weapons or tools. Out of this use grew the idea that arrow-heads were potent charms in providing bodily protection against enemy force or the usual illnesses. Accordingly, people began to wear them as neck ornaments and, for this purpose, decorative arrow-heads were made. Ever since then, they have been cherished for their powers in warding off attacks, and a superstition still exists which claims that if one of these arrow-heads is dipped in water, the water will be more potent than any doctor's medicine.

THE CADUCEUS.—This device, which figures as part of the design of some postage stamps, has been considered a bringer of good fortune ever since the time of the ancient Greeks. It consists of two snakes entwining a rod, surmounted by a pine cone. By the side of the cone is a pair of wings. It was the symbol of Mercury. The rod had the supernatural powers of

No. 4.—The Caduceus or Staff of Mercury.

quelling disputes and letting people dwell in harmony. The snakes possessed the property of healing; the pine cone preserved good health; and the wings stood for speed and progress. Thus people wear the caduceus today in order to ensure a life free from quarrels and illness, and to enable them to be healthy and "go ahead."

THE EYE AGATE.—As is generally appreciated, the "evil eye" is the source of all trouble and misfortunes, and the early Eastern races thought that, if the "evil eye" could be avoided or frightened away, all would be well. Searching for a charm to effect their purpose, they alighted upon the eye agate, and this they believed would give no quarter to the "evil eye." Accordingly, agates were cut to resemble an eye which would be powerful enough to neutralize the effects of the evil one, and these were worn as brooches, rings and necklaces. The agate chosen for the purpose consisted of thin layers of stone of various colors. Thus, by cutting the stones oval and removing parts of the top layers, it was possible to produce a charm closely resembling a human eye, both in shape and color.

Such eyes are still sold today, and many people treasure them in the hope that they will ward off evil in any form.

THE JADE AXE-HEAD.—Many jewelers still sell little axe-heads carved out of jade, for wearing around the neck. The axe-head has been considered a symbol of strength and vigor ever since primitive times, and jade has a world-wide reputation as a charm against disease and accidents.

THE SEAL OF SOLOMON.—This device is now regarded as a symbol of the Jewish religion, but it can be traced to several other religions, and, no doubt, it dates even farther back than the commencement of the Jewish era. The triangle with the upward point stood for goodness; the triangle

No. 5.—The Seal of Solomon, one of the oldest lucky charms in existence.

with the downward point for wickedness; while the two intertwined symbolized the triumph of good over bad. Those who wear the device contend that it preserves them from all that is ill, and, at the same time, it gives them a share of the world's blessings.

THE ABRACADABRA.—This charm dates from the second century, and was a symbol of the Gnostic worship. It often took the form of a little piece of parchment, folded into the shape of a cross, but it can, also, be seen as a tablet, made of stone or metal, shaped like an inverted triangle. On the charm, of whatever shape, was inscribed the following:

```
A B R A C A D A B R A
  B R A C A D A B R
    R A C A D A B
      A C A D A
        C A D
          A
```

It will be seen that the word "Abracadabra" can be read along the upper line and also down and up the two sides. This word is said to conceal the name of God and the charm has the powers of warding off dangers and sickness.

THE FOUR-LEAF CLOVER OR SHAMROCK.—Everyone knows that a four-leaf clover or shamrock is supposed to be a bringer of luck and good fortune. As these are not readily found and, moreover, they soon perish, the opportunity has been seized by jewelers to produce artificial ones in various precious and semi-precious metals. To wear either is supposed to avoid misfortune. It may be mentioned that the four-leaf Shamrock as a charm has proved immensely popular by those who are interested in the Irish sweepstakes.

BLACK CATS.—Of course, it is lucky for a black cat to walk into your house, but failing an actual cat, a counterfeit one serves the same purpose. Thus, people who pin their faith to black cats often make stuffed ones, or draw pictures of them, and look to the creature of their own handiwork to serve the role of mascot.

YOUR OWN TALISMAN.—So far, the talismans that have received universal acceptance have alone been mentioned, but the tendency today is for enthusiasts to originate a mascot of their very own. It may take any or every form, according to the whim or fancy of the individual. Maybe you will prefer to find your own mascot or talisman in this direction. If you have no preferences, why not constitute a device which embraces your lucky number, your lucky flower, your lucky color, and so on? It is a suggestion bristling with opportunities.

Just to show that people are tending towards the idea of choosing a talisman of their very own, we will conclude with a story that was recently published.

"There is a precious stone to which the board of directors of a firm of diamond dealers annually pass a vote of thanks. The stone is a sapphire and it has been named Shani, meaning 'bringer of luck.'

"Shani was bought by the firm about seventy years ago, and it only leaves the safe on New Year's Day. A special meeting, attended by every member of the firm, is then held in the board room. Shani is placed in the middle of the table and, with hands clasped in prayer, the members offer thanks for the good luck the sapphire has brought the firm during the preceding year.

"One of the directors said, 'My grandfather once received a tempting offer for Shani and yielded, but a few hours after the sapphire had been sent away he was taken violently ill with fever. The sapphire was brought back from a distant part of India, and my grandfather became well at once.'"

Should not we all have a Shani?

HINTS ON FORTUNETELLING

HUNDREDS of dollars are paid each week to professional fortunetellers by people in all walks of life, in order that they may gain a peep into the future. These people belong to every class of society; they are of all ages and they consult the mediums on almost every matter connected with human existence. There is the industrial magnate, the society girl, and the hard-working shop assistant, all anxious to peer into the coming months.

Accordingly, the teller of fortunes and the writer of horoscopes is doing an excellent business. The dollars and the cents are pouring in at a remarkable rate, and those who read the future, as a profession, are having the time of their lives.

This state of things is one calculated to make you stop and think for a moment. Why should not you learn the rudiments of fortunetelling yourself? Why should not you find out how to read the signs of your own future and the future of your friends? The subject is interesting; it is not a difficult one and all you need to know is set out in this book.

Your course of study may well begin with the chapter on Palmistry. Having mastered that, turn to the one on Handwriting, and follow with *"What do your Bumps Mean?"* These three sections will give you a very useful start and then you might continue with *"How Astrology Decides Your Destiny"* and *"Your Face is Your Fortune."*

The five chapters named will enable you to read people with a great deal of success, and it should not be long before your friends compliment you on your accuracy. Probably this will spur you to further efforts, and you will study the passages on lucky numbers, dreams, tea-cup readings, lucky colors, etc. These will add a polish to your preliminary knowledge.

Very soon you will gain a reputation as a seer and it will add not a little to your vanity when people come to you and ask you to read their futures. In doing so, you will be advised to follow a few rules. Never jump to hasty conclusions. Weigh all the facts and strike a balance. If the hand says "yes" and the face says "no," the conclusion is that "it may be." When disappointing things are noted, be charitable and let the applicant off lightly. In cases where dire illnesses are portended, suppress the facts or state them in such a way that the applicant has a chance of avoiding the trouble, if he or she takes suitable measures. But, whatever happens, never make a statement for which you have not "chapter and verse."

And this brings me to my last point. Hands, faces, heads and other characteristics give their readings, but none of these readings should be taken as absolutely final. The power is within us to fight against our failings and to better our good qualities. We may even allow our best ones to deteriorate. That is why two people born at the same time and in the same town need not grow up exactly alike. And it is also why a small percentage of horoscopes and fortunes are bound to miss the mark.

PALMISTRY—WHAT MAY BE LEARNED
FROM HANDS

"There are more things in Heaven and Earth . . . "

People who can see as far as the ends of their noses and then only through a fog, declare (with a superior sniff) that Palmistry is nothing but a trap to catch fools; they call it quackery, or declare perhaps that it is merely a fake or blind guesswork.

Now, while we would be the first to deny that Palmistry is an exact and infallible science, yet we just as strongly affirm that it is undoubtedly a most fascinating and interesting recreation; as to its truth, each one must decide that question for himself.

For the few who have a wish to take up this study seriously, there are many now who will naturally wish to know just sufficient to be able to "tell fortunes." Fortunetellers are always popular at some jolly party or quiet friendly gathering of an evening.

In this book they will find all the simple information required; on the other hand the student will find a sincere delight in reading and sifting thoroughly the numerous books that probe the depths of the subject.

Quite apart from any markings which may be upon the hand, a general indication of the habits and temperament of the individual in question can readily be gained by a careful examination of the texture or quality of the skin.

It were as well to note here that the impressions gained must never be taken by themselves, but only in conjunction with other confirming signs. Especially is this so when judging the character of a friend or acquaintance.

TEXTURE OF SKIN.—The skin may, of course, be smooth or rough. To judge this you should turn the hand in question back upwards; now get the feel of the skin by actual touch; a smooth, fine-textured skin denotes a refined nature, and *vice versa*. This is a very strong indication indeed, insomuch that should there be other tendencies pointing to coarseness of nature, this texture of the hand would have a refining effect upon the whole.

ELASTICITY OF THE HAND.—This is best tested by actual grip (as in shaking hands). All hands naturally present some feeling of elasticity; this is a matter of comparison, but it is very easy to tell the quick, virile grip of an elastic hand to the dead fish feeling which a flabby hand gives us when we grasp it.

A FLEXIBLE HAND denotes an active and energetic person, one who will be readily adaptable to new conditions. He will always rise to the occasion, and manfully withstands the buffets of ill-fortune. This type is always trustworthy and a good friend.

13

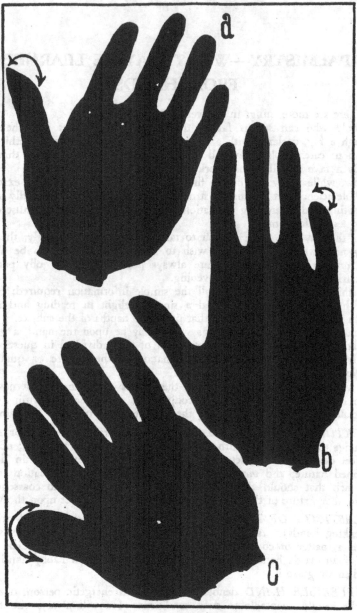

No. 6.—Beware of these Hands.—A shows a weak, flattened thumb; B a curved little finger and C a coarse, short thumb. Each has other defects as well.

A FLABBY HAND—one that does not respond to your grip or responds but sluggishly—is the hand of an idle man, untrustworthy and inconsistent, a man of weak and negative character; but be sure to search well for other confirming signs of this weakness.

THE SHAPE OF THE HAND

A fairly accurate guide to character is certainly contained in the shape of the hand. Hands may be roughly divided into two classes—broad and long. A person having a *long hand* you may judge to have great capacity for mental effort and matters of detail.

The broad-handed person you may expect to be a strong man physically; his culture will be bodily rather than mental. He could with advantage improve his culture by reading, and by enjoying the best music.

THE SHAPE OF THE FINGERS

When an individual is found with *square* finger-tips, he should make a good marriage partner; he will be practical—a man of method and reason. He is punctual, but should cultivate imagination.

POINTED FINGER tips will be found on the hand of the musician, the painter, and, in fact, anyone who is of artistic temperament.

Persons with these fingers should curb their imagination with reason, and cultivate the power of doing things, not only dreaming them, though dreaming is well enough in its way.

TAPERING fingers indicate people of extremes. "Ice and fire" are these people—impulsive and generous to a fault. They should guard against undue and morbid sensitiveness, and should cultivate a sane philosophical outlook upon life. They are capable of the highest, but are frequently their own worst enemies.

SPATULATE FINGERS.—These are the sportsmen of the world. They are not worried much by the opinions of others, while they love a busy, healthy life; a sound mind in a sound body.

GENERAL SHAPE AND FORMATION OF THE HAND

If the hands are knotted with the joints swollen, powers of analysis, calculation and reflection are shown; philosophers have this type of hand.

SMOOTH fingers and hands indicate the artistic temperament. These people are frequently inspired, and have curious intuitions concerning coming events. Musicians, spiritualists, and martyrs are of this type, together with many folk who are square pegs in round holes; maybe doing work which is uncongenial to them.

THE THUMB has also in it certain very marked indications of character. The three bones (or Phalanges) in the thumb each have their interpretation. Beginning at the top these should be judged by length as follows:—

1. Will. (The pushing type of man.)
2. Reasoning power. (The thinker or philosopher.)
3. Love.

Thus a long first or top phalange indicates great will power; or if it is not a certain indication, it points to a definite likelihood of the will being strong.

THE MOUNTS

Take your subject's hand and examine it closely; a strong magnifying glass should form part of the equipment of every wise palmist. It will be seen that there are certain portions of the hands which are raised above the surface. These are known as "mounts." As will be noticed in the accompanying picture, we call these mounts by astrological names, a method adopted from the very earliest times. They are eight in number, named: Jupiter, Mercury, Venus, Saturn, Apollo, Luna and Mars (of which there are two).

Let us look at our picture on page 21. At the base of the first finger you will see Mount Jupiter, then taking the base of each finger in turn, will be found Mounts Saturn, Apollo, and Mercury. Mount Luna will be found at the base of the hand, below the little finger, near the wrist, Mount Mars just above it, Mount Venus stands below Jupiter and at the root of the thumb, with the second Mars above it.

All individuals have not these mounts developed to the same extent, and in these variations strong indications of character are to be found.

We will now have a little discussion upon the subject of Mounts, taking each individually, and in turn.

Usually one of these mounts in your subject's hands will be found to stand out clearly from the remainder. This will give you a good idea of the general type of person whose hand you are judging.

These are the general indications to be found.

THE SATURNIAN.—If the Mount of Saturn be over-developed, you have the cold, sceptical type of man. He lacks the milk of human kindness, and is probably a pessimist. A moderate development, on the other hand, is good; this man should be prudent, not miserly; optimistic yet not fatuously so, a well-balanced man.

We well know that the excess or over-development of one particular quality (however excellent this quality may be) is evil. Thus a super-artistic temperament gives the neurotic; while the over-prudent man becomes the grasping miser.

THE JUPITERIAN.—Jupiterians, or folk with an excessively strong mount of this name, are the strong men of the world. In excess they are ambitious to a fault, masterful, overbearing and bullying. With a moderate development we have exceedingly good qualities indicated. Power of leadership, rightful ambition, initiative, and great abilities for hard work.

THE APOLLONIAN.—Taking the men and women of Apollo we have the essential optimists, the Micawbers and Mark Tapleys of life. Allied to their cheery natures is a love of the artistic and the really beautiful. The sculptors, painters, and musicians who make life so pleasant, are very frequently Apollonians. The best advice to give an Apollonian is "moderation in all things." He or she must be very careful in the choice of a marriage partner; this last is very important indeed.

THE MERCURIAN.—In excess we have craft, guile, and fondness for falsehoods. In moderation we find the good business man, shrewd, cautious, possessor of a capacity for doing the lion's share of the work, and a fine eye for the main chance. Let him cultivate his opposites. Unselfishness, kindness and generosity will make a Mercurian a most charming person. Their lack will leave a clever, scheming scoundrel.

THE MARTIAN.—When we find Mars in the ascendant (i. e., the mounts excessively developed) we find aggression and even bullying. In moderation we have a fighter in the best sense of the word; a man who will withstand the blows of fate and fight his way through life, resisting evil. He is never mean, and you will find him a sincere and trustworthy friend.

THE VENUSIAN.—When this mount is predominant in excess we find a person of unbalanced mind; he will be careless and will make a dangerous marriage partner. Developed to a moderate degree we find generosity, a power to feel for others, with a pleasing personality. The folk of Venus love beauty, and love their life; they are strongly attracted to those of the opposite sex, and are likely to fall in love without counting the cost. These people should cultivate a habit of thinking before they act, and should not allow generosity to degenerate into extravagance.

THE LUNARIAN.—Lastly let us take the Mount of the Moon. In excess we again find the neurotic or unduly nervous person. In moderation the Lunarian will be a person of imagination, sympathy, and one who loves to look on all that is most beautiful in life. He should be successful as a musician, playwright, or novelist, and has a ready capacity for learning foreign languages.

Let me give one piece of final advice to those who truly judge character by the mounts, or indeed by any signs on the hand. Never judge by one sign or you will be led into stupid mistakes. Always take the hand as a whole, for frequently some point in the formation striking you as bad may be strongly counterbalanced by other good signs.

This is exceedingly important, and rightly applied will save you many foolish pitfalls in your early fortunetelling days!

THE FINGERS

Each of the mounts at the base of the fingers gives its name to the finger above it, i. e., the first finger is called Jupiter, the little finger is Mercury, and so on.

When judging character by the mounts, the fingers which share their name must also always be noted as to their development. Let us first take Jupiter.

If that finger is well developed (i. e., long in comparison to the remainder) this will accentuate the Jupiterian qualities seen in the well-developed mounts. This may be applied throughout the mounts. The important thing to remember is that mount and corresponding finger should be read together. This is essential.

To conclude this section let us take the phalanges (or joints of the finger) with their interpretations.

Counting from the top joint nearest to the nail, the meaning given by palmists to the three phalanges of each finger are as follows:—

(*Length of phalanx,* or distance between the respective joints, is the *deciding factor.*) For simplicity, we have made a small table.

Name of Finger	1st Joint.	2nd Joint.	3rd Joint.
JUPITER	Religion.	Ambition.	Despotic or fondness for governing others.
SATURN	Fondness for spiritual mysticism.	Out-door life.	Earthly ambition.
APOLLO	Excess or foolish optimism (Micawber).	Caution.	Love of show.
MERCURY	The orator's finger.	Great tenacity.	Cunning and greed.

THE LINES OF YOUR DESTINY

We now come to the most fascinating side of Palmistry—the actual study of the network of lines upon the hand, and their relation to the mounts and to each other.

This is where your magnifying glass will be of enormous value. There are very many small signs, seemingly of little matter, but in reality of very great importance, such as stars, crosses, squares, and triangles, little marks with frequently great meanings.

One word of warning must be given before we go farther. If you see evil in a palm never on any account tell of it. But if you see some misfortune approaching which a little foresight might avoid, by all means warn your subject. Should you by any chance see, or think you see, anything calculated to alarm another, keep it to yourself. Always remember that human intelligence is frail and finite but life is infinite. Palmistry shares in this frailty; it is interesting and intensely fascinating, but far from infallible. It is not an exact science in the sense of mathematics, where two plus two equals four, no more and no less.

Let us take these lines in turn and discuss the meaning of each.

THE LIFE LINE

When the Life line rises high in the hand, great ambition is shown. If you see a Life line circling well into the palm (thus forming a large Mount of Venus) emotional characteristics such as love and generosity are shown. If, on the contrary, the line forms a small Mount of Venus, coldness will be predominant.

If the Life line commences very feebly and gradually strengthens, this is a good sign. It indicates a weak childhood but a robust maturity.

THE HEAD LINE

The Head line works in conjunction with the line of Health (see illustration), thus:—If the Head line is broken some ill health may be indicated which has made or will make its effect felt upon the brain and thinking powers. But only if all other lines should support this.

An independent nature is shown when the Head line branches off from the Life line early in its course, and vice versa.

If the Head line should curve towards Saturn, there is shown a material outlook upon life; this is the financier's Head line. Curving towards Apollo an artistic nature is shown, while should this line originate near Mount Jupiter it is a sure sign of capacity for leadership, and many go-ahead qualities that make for success. If the Head line is firm, a definite, purposeful nature is probable, while a weak, wavy Head line indicates a weak, wavering outlook upon life.

With the Head line joining the Heart line, emotional qualities are to the fore; this individual is impulsive and should put the curb of reason upon himself.

Should the Head line have branches which run towards Mount Mercury, Luna and Mars, it is an excellent sign, showing good balance, ready wit, and quick adaptability.

THE HEART LINE

When this originates on or near the mount called Saturn, there is a leaning towards a sensual, pleasure-loving nature.

Rising from between Saturn and its neighbor Jupiter, we have a very deliberate, practical man. His love, while very sincere, is governed by reason; he is intensely practical, and rather lacking in imagination, which it were well worth his while to cultivate. His head will always rule his Heart, especially is this indicated should the Heart line bend towards that of the Head.

Should the Heart line cross the palm entirely, the owner is the exact opposite of the individual just mentioned. This person's heart will rule his head; he is sentimental even to a fault, and should practice business-like qualities, and not dream overmuch. Love in a cottage is all very well— but how when the roof leaks?

A short Heart line is a warning for care in marriage; without this care a couple may well come to shipwreck on the rocks of married life. Forewarned is forearmed!

THE LINE OF FORTUNE

This is a line running (as its name suggests) towards the Mount of Apollo. It is a valuable and somewhat rarely-found line. This is the line of genius; effort will scarcely be needed by its owner; he will seem to fly towards success on the wings of destiny.

This is the ideal, but it must be borne in mind that there are other lines which must be studied in conjunction with it.

On the other hand its absence does by no means prohibit or even endanger success; it merely indicates that individual effort will be required, and what is life without something to strive for?

THE HEALTH LINE

A good strong Health line is very desirable; should this line be broken, however, there is no need for alarm, it is merely indicated that a certain amount of care is necessary in one's personal habits of life.

THE LINE OF FATE

This line runs across the middle of the palm, from the Mount of Saturn to the Bracelets, but its full course need not be traced on any particular hand. When of full length and a middle position is revealed, the fate of the individual may be reckoned as particularly lucky. Such a person has strong determination, can make quick decisions and can be powerful without being a tyrant. He has the power of drawing people to him, in a friendly way, and is, thus, always liked.

Should the line run from the Bracelets and stop at the Head line, this is a sign that the possessor will have many troubles and obstacles to overcome. Whether he will surmount them depends on the strength of the Head line. In cases where the Fate line continues up one of the fingers, the owner must take care that success does not turn his head and ruin the future. A Fate line that wriggles its way across the palm indicates a life of ups and downs,

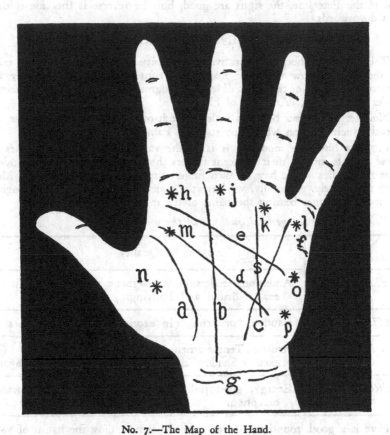

No. 7.—The Map of the Hand.

a. Life line;
b. Fate line;
c. Health line;
d. Head line;
e. Heart line;
f. Marriage line;
g. Bracelets;

h. Mount of Jupiter;
j. Mount of Saturn:
k. Mount of Apollo;
l. Mount of Mercury:
m. and o. Mounts of Mars;
n. Mount of Venus;
p. Mount of Luna;
s. Line of Fortune.

and, should the line be broken in places, it is a sign that happiness will vary from time to time. Generally speaking, if small lines run upwards out of the Fate line, the signs are good, but the reverse is the case if they run downwards.

THE LINE OF MARRIAGE

This line is a short, comparatively inconspicuous one, found at the edge of the palm, below the little finger. It runs inwards but not very far towards the center of the palm. How to recognize its significance is explained under the heading, "An ABC of Hands."

Now let us put our house in order, refresh our minds, and summarize the broad principles upon which any study of Palmistry must rest.

First we have the mounts. It is in the varying relation of the lines to these mounts and to their adjacent fingers that our deductions are founded. One mount lies at the base of each finger, Jupiter, Saturn, Apollo and Mercury respectively. Secondly, we have the four fingers with their astrological names, each finger bearing the name of the mount at its base.

Table showing the general qualities of the mounts.

Name of Mount	Quality
JUPITER	Ambition, leadership, a magnetic personality. (In excess) Brutal and bullying.
SATURN	Cautious, prudent. (In excess) Miserliness, coldness.
APOLLO	Artistic Temperament, optimist, healthy living. (In excess) Shallow character, frivolous, and extravagant.
MERCURY	Energy, good judgment. (In excess) Lying, fraud, deception.

Here is a good, sound rule to remember when reading the hands of your friends. First find your type—i.e., Jupiterian, Apollonian, etc. This is accomplished by noting the main characteristics of the hand which you are examining. Suppose that the Mount of Apollo is fully developed and well raised, and that the finger of Apollo is inclined to be long, there you have practically a pure Apollonian type, i.e., Apollo in excess. If the Mount of Apollo is developed but also the finger of Saturn is long, this forms an admirable mixture. This subject will feel the benefit of the steadying influence of Saturn at work on his light-hearted Apollonian nature.

Pure types are rare—and fortunately so—for in a pure type, no matter which, you are frequently liable to find a rather poorly-balanced outlook on life. The cold need heat, and the brilliant require solid perseverence and a capacity for hard work to win lasting success.

No. 8.—The Marriage Line in varying shapes.

WHICH HAND SHOULD BE READ?

The answer to this question is a very decided both! As a general rule the left hand will show the inherent characteristics of the individual; the right hand shows the same characteristics modified by our surroundings or by the individual's personal efforts. The former is possibility—the latter actuality; in short, it is what we actually make our life.

The safest rule about reading right and left hands is this:—Read both hands separately and carefully, then read them in their relation one to the other.

There is no blind fatalism in the sayings and doings of a true student of Palmistry. What he does or should do is to point out the likelihoods and warn against inherent weakness. In so much he is like a guide helping us to pick our way through the tortuous maze of life.

It may strike some of our readers that we have spoken more of the indications of character to be found in the hand rather than of the indications of "Fortune." A few moments' thought will show a very sound reason for this.

It is certainly our characters which shape our destinies; should you find a hand with all the indications of strong character, while also possessing a strong will and well-cut Life line, you would be sure in prophesying a happy life for its owner; or as sure as we poor humans ever can hope to be!

If you find a hand with the indications of weak will and character, yet with the Health and Life lines strong and well defined, you may well advise the owner of the hand that effort, effort and effort again, is required if he or she would win through!

Remember that tact is more precious than fine gold! A tactful and timely warning may prove of the greatest value, while without tact you will surround yourself with an army of acquaintances whose feelings you have hurt by your thoughtless and unintentionally cruel remarks!

There is no infallibility about this matter, but with the facts given in this book there are vast possibilities for really pleasurable and interesting recreation. If the study be taken up seriously, and used with discretion, there are almost unbelievable opportunities for good.

This is what a man once said to me—and he was a man who thought deeply, and probed matters to their depths:

"A wise palmist is as precious as a careful signalman upon life's crowded railroad, and a wise palmist is a tactful palmist."

AN A B C OF HANDS

In order to be able to follow the explanations given for each type of hand, the list set out below will prove useful.

(1) The 1st phalange is the section of the finger carrying the nail.

(2) The 2nd phalange is the section of the finger between the 1st and 2nd joints.

(3) The 3rd phalange is the section of the finger between the 2nd and 3rd joints.

(4) The positions of the Mounts of Mercury, Apollo, Saturn, Jupiter, Luna and Venus are shown in Fig. 7. Of the Mounts of Mars, there are two positions. One is situated between the Mount of Jupiter and the thumb, while the other comes between the Mounts of Mercury and Luna.

(5) The Girdle of Venus, which is rarely found, is a curved line running between Mercury and either Jupiter or Saturn.

(6) The Bracelets are the lines running across the wrist, close to where it joins the palm.

ABILITY.—A small cross is shown where the Life line finishes.

ABILITY, LACK OF.—A short Head line, terminating in the center of the palm, with the Mounts of Saturn and Apollo almost non-existing.

ACTIVE PERSON.—A rough, firm palm and an indistinct Heart line.

AFFECTIONATE PERSON.—A clear Heart line and a very plump Mount of Apollo.

AMBITIOUS PERSON.—A short line traced from the Life line to the Mount of Jupiter, existing on both hands.

AMIABLE PERSON.—The Mounts of Jupiter and Mercury are very plump on both palms.

AMOROUS PERSON.—A hand deeply furrowed, somewhat silky in texture and the Heart line well developed.

ANGER.—The thumb has short phalanges, especially the first phalange; finger-nails square and reddish at the base.

ARTISTIC TEMPERAMENT.—A line running directly from the Head line to the third finger, and fingers long and tapering.

AUDACIOUS PERSON.—The Mount of Mercury and the two Mounts of Mars very clearly in evidence.

AVARICIOUS.—The Head line extends across the palm, from end to end, and is straight. At its end, it forms a small triangle.

BILIOUS TEMPERAMENT.—The Health line wriggles its way along the palm, while the hand is damp and clammy.

BRAVE PERSON.—Straight fingers and both the Mounts of Mars are well defined. Few hair lines cut across these mounts.

CAUTIOUS PERSON.—The first phalange of the thumb twists inwards, whilst all the fingers are remarkably straight.

CHARITABLE PERSON.—A good Heart line with well-developed Mounts of Venus and Mars (particularly the Mars Mount below Jupiter.)

CHEERFUL PERSON.—A long first phalange to the fourth finger and the Mounts of Jupiter, Apollo and Mercury nice and plump.

CLEVER PERSON.—The Life line shows a cross at one of its ends and the Mounts of Apollo and Mercury are well defined.

CONCEITED PERSON.—Very plump Mounts of Saturn, Apollo and Mercury.

CONSCIENTIOUS PERSON.—A broad, thin hand, a very distinct Mount of Jupiter, and the first phalange of the thumb nicely curved.

CONVINCING SPEAKER.—The fourth finger is almost as long as the third, usually because the first phalange is long. This finger is pointed.

CORDIALITY.—The Heart line extends almost across the palm; it is straight, except at one end, which branches into a fork.

COWARDLY.—When the hand is opened out flat, the fourth phalanges of all the fingers dip or curve downwards. None of the mounts are distinct.

CRUEL PERSON.—The Heart line is almost or quite non-existing. The hand is long, but square-cornered, and the finger-nails are pointed at the base.

DARING PERSON.—The Heart line curves round to the back of the hand, while both the Mounts of Mars are fully developed.

DECEITFUL PERSON.—The Head line wavers, is not very distinct, and it has a double prong at one end. One of the prongs cuts across the Mount of Luna.

DEFIANT PERSON.—The third phalange of the first finger is longer than the third phalanges of other fingers. The thumb is large.

DISAPPOINTMENTS TO BE EXPERIENCED.—The Life line has a number of small hair lines running from it, like herringbone pattern. Some of these hair lines reach the bracelets.

DISSIPATED PERSON.—A star beside the thumb-nail and the Head line is deep and wide.

ENERGETIC PERSON.—The head line runs from side to side of the palm. It is clear throughout, while the four mounts below the four fingers are very distinct.

ENVIOUS PERSON.—On the first finger there are several clear lines; they are found mostly on the third phalange, but some exist on the second. None on the first.

EXTRAVAGANT PERSON.—The tips of all the fingers bend back and the Head line is weak.

FAITHLESS PERSON.—The two Mounts of Mars and that of Mercury stand out more clearly than the others.

FAME, PERSON DESTINED FOR.—The Fate line is more distinct than any other and no other line crosses it.

FAR-SEEING PERSON.—The palm is depressed in the middle, the thumb is well developed, strong in outline, and all the phalanges of the fingers are about as long as they are wide.

FAULT-FINDING PERSON.—A long, narrow hand, with an ill-defined Heart line.

FLIRT.—The Head line consists of a line joining up several links, forming a species of chain.

FORCEFUL PERSON.—A cross on the Mount of Apollo and small lines crossing.

FORTUNATE PERSON.—The Heart and Head lines almost touch below the Mount of Jupiter. A cross is often found between them just at this point. The third finger shows a long line running the length of two phalanges.

GOOD CHARACTER.—The Mounts of Jupiter, Saturn and Mercury are much in evidence, while the tips of the fingers are nicely rounded.

GREEDY PERSON.—When the hand is spread out the fingers bend inwards, because of the excessive width of the palm. The Head line runs across the palm almost in a straight line.

HAPPY PERSON.—On the third finger there is a deep line running the length of the third phalange. Also, the bracelets appear as a single deep furrow.

HARD WORKER.—The fourth finger has the second phalange a trifle long, while the two Mounts or Mars are well developed.

IDLER.—The Head line is very short; the Mounts of Luna and Mercury are well developed, while the Mount of Mercury almost touches that of Mars.

IMPATIENT PERSON.—The Mounts of Mars and Mercury stand well above the level of the palm and are crossed by several small lines.

INTELLIGENT PERSON.—The Mounts of Apollo and Mercury are much in evidence, while the Life line terminates in a cross.

JEALOUS PERSON.—The Head line continues round to the back of the hand, while the Mount of Mercury is more defined than the others.

JUST PERSON.—Square-tipped fingers and square nails, while the space formed between the Heart and Head lines is unusually wide.

KIND PERSON.—A star figures on the thumb, while the Mounts of Apollo and Mercury are much in evidence. The Heart line is not short.

LIKING FOR OPPOSITE SEX.—A star is seen on the Mount of Mercury or a star may appear between the Heart and Head lines.

LONG LIFE.—The Heart line curves entirely round the thumb, being plainly evident all the way, while the bracelets consist of three clear lines.

LUCKY PERSON.—See diagram of a very lucky hand.

MARRIAGE.—The Marriage line is a comparatively short line, found above the Heart line and starting from the edge of the palm, under the little finger.

If straight and well defined, it is a sign of a happy married life. (See Fig. A, p. 23.)

If curved down, there are troubles to overcome.

If the line runs down to the Heart line, money difficulties will arise in married life. (See Fig. B.)

If the line ends in a fork, there are fears of quarrels and, perhaps, separations. (See Fig. C.)

If the line runs up and touches the Fate line, marriage will bring many successes.

If there is practically no length to the actual marriage line, but a fork appears almost at the commencement, it is a clear proof that troubles will arise and prevent the owner from marrying when he or she desires it. There will be delays, postponements and other difficulties, but they will be overcome in the end. (See Fig. D.)

If there is an island where the line should commence, this may be taken as a sign that the possessor is not a suitable person for marriage. But, if the line is a good one, after the island is past, there are hopes that he or she will mend. (See Fig. E.)

If the marriage line hardly exists or does not appear at all, it is a sign of single blessedness through life.

If the marriage line on the right hand is minutely examined, short hair lines may be seen rising upwards from it. The number of these denotes the number of children of the marriage. It is usually said that the perpendicular lines represent the boys and the slanting lines the girls. As these lines are often very indistinct, it may be necessary to dust the hand with a dab of face-powder, in order to see them.

NARROW-MINDED PERSON.—The Head line is short and it wavers or wriggles its way across the palm.

NEAT, ORDERLY PERSON.—Where each finger is hinged to the palm, there is a deep crease making a badge on either side of it. The hand itself is square and vigorous in appearance.

NERVOUS PERSON.—The hand is very much lined, and there is difficulty in picking out the chief lines. The Mount of Luna is large and much furrowed.

A VERY LUCKY HAND

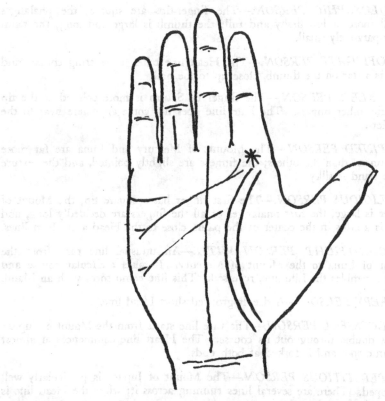

No. 9.—*The Life line begins on the Mount of Jupiter and is doubled.* The Heart line commences on the same mount and is forked at both ends. The Head line is doubled and forked at one end. The Fate line is long, straight and rises from the Bracelets. The finger of Apollo is lined. The Marriage line is straight and clear.

OVERBEARING PERSON.—The fingers are square-tipped and the first phalange of the thumb is long and thick. The hand itself is rough and coarse. A short Heart line.

PASSIONATE PERSON.—The Heart line is long and the Mount of Mercury over-pronounced.

PHILOSOPHIC PERSON.—The finger-tips are square; the phalanges are all more or less fleshy and full; the thumb is large and long; the palm is comparatively small.

PROFLIGATE PERSON.—The Head line takes a wavering course, and there is a star on the thumb, close up to the nail.

RECKLESS PERSON.—The finger of Saturn is more pointed at the tip than the other fingers. The Fate line does not come anywhere near to the Bracelets.

REFINED PERSON.—The Mounts of Mercury and Luna are far more pronounced than the others; the fingers are slightly pointed, and the texture of the hand is silky.

RELIGIOUS PERSON.—The first finger has a square tip; the Mount of Jupiter is large; the first phalanges of all the fingers are decidedly long, and there is a cross in the center of the palm, close to the Head and Heart lines.

SECOND-SIGHT, PERSON WITH.—An unusual line runs from the Mount of Luna to the Mount of Mercury. It takes a circular course and much resembles the Life line, reversed. This line commences with an island.

SLEEPY PERSON.—A deeply-grooved short Head line.

SUCCESSFUL PERSON.—The Life line starts from the Mount of Jupiter and is double throughout its course. The Heart line commences at almost the same spot and is forked at both ends.

SUPERSTITIOUS PERSON.—The Mount of Jupiter is particularly well developed. There are several lines running across it; while the Head line is shorter than usual.

TACTFUL PERSON.—The hands are long and narrow; the texture of the skin is smooth and silky, and all the first phalanges are plump and, perhaps, longitudinally lined.

TALKATIVE PERSON.—The Heart and Head lines are not easily discovered, and the Mount of Mercury stands up more than the other mounts.

THOUGHTFUL PERSON.—The first finger almost as long as the second; it is pointed at the tip more than the others. A wide space is formed between the Heart, Head, Fate and Fortune (or Health) lines.

TIMID PERSON.—None of the Mounts appear plainly, while the Head and Heart lines run very close together.

UNTRUTHFUL PERSON.—The little finger is long, reaching at least to the base of the nail of the third finger. The Mount of Luna is crossed with many lines.

VAIN PERSON.—The Mount of Jupiter is fuller than the others and it is crossed with many lines. The fingers are long and rather pointed.

VINDICTIVE PERSON.—The Head line wriggles along its course. It has a fork close to the Mount of Luna.

WEALTHY PERSON.—When earned, the Mount of Luna, on both hands, shows a number of lines which all run in one direction. They do not cross at all. When inherited, the same, but there is, in addition, a cross on the Bracelets.

WITTY PERSON.—The Mount of Mercury shows up clearly. In addition, there is a curved line which runs from the junction of the first and second fingers to the junction of the third and fourth fingers. The Heart line is usually good.

YOUR HANDWRITING REVEALS
YOUR CHARACTER

Your handwriting is you; disguise it as you will, it still reveals your character. As a matter of fact, it is a sheer impossibility for an ordinary person to alter his or her writing completely. The natural hand and the purposely-changed hand will bear several resemblances, however hard the individual may try to make them dissimilar. This is due to the fact that the same character lies behind both efforts. Not only is your handwriting you, but the handwriting of your friend is "him or her." This being so, you will find it a simple matter to arrive at his or her qualities by analyzing a few lines of the person's handwriting. To become sufficiently expert for this, you will not need more than half-an-hour's study.

FIRST of all we must attend to the direction of the lines of writing, as, should these be level, a normal and calm state of mind is shown, generally reliable, and not subject to change.

When the lines slope toward the right, much energy is indicated; when the lines slope downward; a lack of energy is shown, usually from depression which may result from ill health.

If the writing slopes upward with excess, it shows recklessness; if downwards, with a very sloping inclination, it shows mental depression verging almost on loss of reason.

If the signature slopes upwards, then we may expect to find personal ambition, but if downwards, some physical weakness. If instead of the whole line ascending only words here and there will ascend, this indicates "hope," but if scattered words ascend and descend in the same line, we may read a lack of tenacity in emotions.

SECONDLY.—The lines forming the letters may appear:—

    (A) Practically upright; or

    (B) Sloping slightly to the right.

    (C) Sloping very much to the right as if each letter were falling over the rest.

    (D) Sloping to the left, and lastly,

    (E) "Back-hand writing."

Between A and B might be called normal.

A Shows pluck and self-possession, and, if pointed, mathematics.

B Tenderness, but should the writing be pointed, a quick, acute mind, with no sympathy with sentiment.

C Shows indolence; if with pointed letters, mental power, but should the letters be rounded, mental and physical indolence.

D Shows a love of ease, while

E Looks peculiar and indicates self-consciousness, and, as a rule, hidden sentimentality.

THIRDLY.—The writing small and pointed, we get curiosity; if medium in size, and gradually increasing towards the end of the line, it shows an outspoken nature; should the writing diminsh towards the end of the line we read tact.

If it is fine and threadlike in appearance, it shows a sensitive mind, diplomacy.

Large writing shows promptness, but if the strokes are very fine, we see appreciation of other people's work—a connoisseur.

Small, clear writing shows love of the abstruse, and if the lines are very delicate, a feeling for the mystic. If the writing is extremely small, it shows pettiness of nature, fussiness over unimportant details.

Letters of different sizes show unreliability of nature, exaggerating trifles and ignoring more important things.

Light and fine writing means delicacy of feeling, but if carried to excess it shows fastidiousness.

FOURTHLY.—The connections of the letters with each other must be judged. If the connecting stroke is long, it shows some facility in talking and expression, the power of using words well, *not* talkativeness.

Letters ingeniously connected show constructiveness, but should they be separate, we get perception and intuition.

Any eccentricity indicates that the person's career has not been ordinary. Marked originality, especially of capitals, shows unusual taste. Tremulous tendency resulting neither from illness nor old age—Irritability. Highly restrained, small—Refractory disposition, difficult to live with. Regular and well-placed lines, followed by those careless and irregular—A mind quick to embark on an enterprise, but lacking perseverance. Back-handed less susceptible than inclined—The head ruling the heart.

Generally the body of the letter or specimen gives the present character, the signature the past.

CROTCHETS.—Egotism, self-satisfaction (a return upon self.)

HARPOONS (HOOKS).—Tenacity, united perhaps with weak will.

DASHES.—Perfectly straight—Persistence.

Undulating.—Art, levity.

Undulating, beginning or finishing with a crotchet or ungraceful flourish.— Lack of taste, slight vulgarity.

Light.—Writer attaches little idea to things expressed.

Ending Thickly.—Resolution, desires ideas to carry weight.

Curved Ascendingly.—Versatility; slight inconsistency; speaks without thought.

Tremulous.—Timidity, hesitation.

Placed at end of line or paragraph.—Lack of self-assertion.

Ending abruptly, thick and hard.—Distrust, reserve.

Sharply elongated.—Impulsive nature; prudence taught by experience.

Used instead of "full stops."—Cultivated caution.

CAPITAL LETTERS.—Large and well-formed.—Pride.

Print-like in shape.—Dignity.

Thin strokes.—Boasting.

Exaggerated in height.—Love of ceremonial.

The angle very pointed.—Acuteness, penetrative, leadership.

Large and badly-formed.—Egomania.

Large upper hall.—Self-assertion.

Large bases.—Self-confidence.

The capital letter of Christian names larger than that of surname.—Love of home.

The capital letter of surname larger.—Love of position.

Small capitals.—Lack of self-assertion.

Capital letters made like small ones.—Said to show poetic feeling, love of Nature.

Print-like in form.—Originality.

Eccentric in any way.—Pose or whim.

Widely spaced.—Love of open air.

Curving far below the line, and almost encircling the word.—Protective love of animals.

Letters incorrectly used.—Small detail made over-important.

Tendency to replace by print.—Sense of form, artistic and poetic.

SPECIAL LETTERS.—A.M.N.H., G.O., R.U.W.—Normal width. —Well-poised mind.

Too wide.—Self-contentment, satisfaction.

Nearly touching.—Timidity, want of knowledge of the world.

First leg slightly raised.—Aristocratic tastes.

Second leg exaggerated.—Pose, affectation.

Unconnected, ending with crotchet rentrant.—Egotistical, selfish.

The letters begun and ended with a small crotchet rentrant.—Avarice, meanness.

Letters and words connected.—Power of assimilating ideas, but lack of originality; logic.

Letters disconnected even with their parts.—Creative power, want of logic.

Equally connected or disconnected.—Balanced intuition and deduction.

Last letter increasing in size.—Lack of power of concealment. Decreasing.
—Finesse.

Handwriting does not invariably show sex, as the qualities indicated are common to both men and women.

The writing develops as the soul develops, and imitation comes before originality.

QUALITIES SHOWN IN HANDWRITING ALPHABETICALLY ARRANGED

ABILITY.—Small writing, angular, clear, decided capitals.

ACCURACY.—Neat, well-placed lines and words, punctuation correct.

AFFECTION.—Softly sloping writing, rounded, fairly thick.

AMIABILITY.—Rounded letters, often unfinished, medium capitals.

AMBITION.—Large first stroke of capital "M's" ascending lines of writing. Imposing signature.

ANALYTICAL.—Small-pointed, clear writing, letters divided, decided capitals.

ARGUMENT.—Words connected, giving logic, and occasional extra long connecting strokes, small writing. (See A.2).

AUTHORITY.—Large capitals, especially the letter "I" and first letter of surname, level crossing to t's.

BOASTFUL.—Large writing, exaggerated capital, flying cross bar to t's. (See A.1.)

BOLD.—Large well-formed capitals, clear rounded, but not pointed writing.

BROAD-MINDED.—Well-spaced words, clear capitals, O's and A's wide and rounded.

CANDOUR.—O's and A's open at the top.

CAPRICE.—Eccentric letters, irregular writing, no punctuation.

CARE.—See Accuracy.

CARELESSNESS.—Ill-formed letters, open O's, no punctuation.

CAUTION.—Dashes used instead of full stops.

CEREMONIOUS.—Capitals important, all large above the line, some added flourishes.

CHANGEABLE.—Letters differently formed, eccentric capitals, variability of line.

CHEERFULNESS.—Short, fat loops, rounded letters.

DEJECTION.—Lines tending downwards, curved letters unfinished, last of capital "M" very small.

DELICACY.—Thin thread-like letters, fine pointed writing. (See A.3.)

DISORDER.—Ill-formed, unfinished letters, no punctuation, separate letters.

DISSIMILATION.—Words terminating in thread-like strokes, interchangeable letters.

DISTRUST.—Last downstroke ending very abruptly.

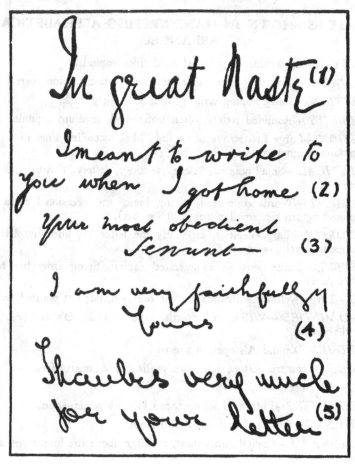

No. 10.—A

DRINK.—Thick strokes, when seen through a glass very ragged, ill-formed letters; self-indulgence.

EATING, GOURMANDIZING.—Small, rounded writing, black, small capitals.

ECONOMY.—Close, compressed writing, no margins. (See A.4.)

ENERGY.—Lines sloping upwards to the right, short downstrokes, high-barred crosses to t's.

EXAGGERATION.—Very large and eccentric capitals, flourish under signature.

EXTRAVAGANCE.—Wide margins, large letters, full loops above and below the lines.

FAINT-HEARTED.—Small capitals, ill-formed thread-like letters, downward tendency.

FOPPERY.—Exaggerated capitals, especially letter "I," wide spacing.

FORGETFULNESS.—Letter "N" shaped like small "U." (See B.1.)

FORMALITY.—Neat lettering, punctuation careful, capitals rather large.

FRIVOLOUS.—Light writing, eccentric, or half-made capitals, irregular lines.

GEOMETRY.—Small, neat writing, print-like small capitals, upright slope to writing, or slightly backward.

GENEROSITY.—Final letters naturally rounded, with upward tendency.

GESTURE OR MOVEMENT.—An elaborate finish resembling a flourish but joined to last letter.

GRANDEUR, LOVE OF.—Imposing and well-formed capitals, large and carefully made "M's."

GROSSNESS.—Very black, thick stroke both up and down, letters badly formed; short loops wide. (See B.2.)

HASTY ACTION.—Long-shaped commas.

HOME, LOVE OF.—Capital letter of Christian name larger than that of surname.

HONESTY.—Well-formed, clear and even letters, level at the bottoms.

HOPE.—The lines ascending with regularity.

HYPOCRISY.—Small A's and O's, open at bottom.

HYSTERIA.—Very irregular writing, badly made letters, and wild crossing strokes to t's, thin and long downstrokes, initial small letters out of proportion to remainder of words.

INDOLENCE.—Rounded writing, sloping "backwards"—i.e., to the left (See A.5.)

INDECISION.—Thin strokes crossing the t's, or else the stroke "tucked in."

INGENUITY.—Curious and original shaped capitals.

INSINCERITY.—Letters raised high above the level, words thread-like, terminations indistinct.

INTEMPERANCE.—Curious rough, black strokes, or else vague formation of letters.

INTRIGUE.—Twisted forms to letters, unnecessary and thread-like strokes.

INTUITION.—Letters separated. (See B.3.)

IRRITABLE.—Curious short downward crossing to t's, cramped and pointed letters.

LANGUAGE.—Occasional long connecting strokes in middle of words or from word to word. (See B.4.)

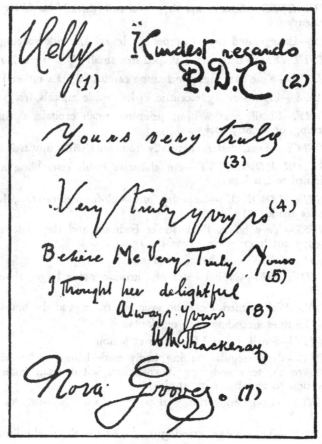

No. 11.—B.

LOGICAL.—Even, small, well-formed letters, capitals well balanced.

LUXURY.—Black writing, slanting strokes, large capitals.

MADNESS.—Irregular, badly-formed, unfinished words, lines very irregular, and variable directions.

MEAN.—Cramped and compressed letters and lines.

METHODICAL.—Well-formed letters, even lines, good punctuation.

NARROW.—Well-formed but close letters, careful capitals.

NATURE, LOVE OF.—Simple capital letters. (See B.5.)

NEUROTIC.—Irregular dwindling letters, various sizes, words unevenly placed.

OBSTINACY.—Small writing, heavy crossing to "t's" and angular letters.

ORDER.—Letters even, well formed and placed.

ORIGINALITY.—Eccentric forms of letters.

PENETRATIVE.—Acute letters, well-finished long upstrokes to "t's."

PERSEVERANCE.—The bars crossing the "t's" increasing in size.

POETRY, FEELING FOR.—Capital letters made like small ones in shape and neat well-formed words.

PRETENTIOUSNESS.—Many curves and involved capitals.

RETICENCE.—Closed "o's," "a's," and "e's."

SIGHT.—In affections of the eyes the terminals are unfinished.

SLY.—Dwindling ill-formed letters.

STINGY.—Cramped writing, close lines.

SUBTLETY.—Small letters and dwindling lines. (See 6.B.)

SELFISH.—The final coming round to the left, and making a complete loop on itself.

TEMPER, HASTY.—Angular stops.

    IRRITABLE.—The cross-bars of the "t's" slightly hooked.

    OBSTINATE.—The cross-bar ending in a decided harpoon or hook; a low thick bar. High and thick and tending sharply downward.

    OBSTINACY AGAINST OWN INTERESTS.—A short straight down stroke.

    CONTROL OF.—Dashes used instead of stops.

TRUE.—Clear, well-formed rounded letters.

VANITY.—Large flourished capitals, wide margins. (See B.7.)

WIT.—Small, rounded letters, generally undulating handwriting.

YOUR FACE IS YOUR FORTUNE

Everybody sums up the faces of his friends and of the people he meets. It is a habit we all have. But most of us are apt to classify these faces into groups according to whether the possessors are good-looking, ordinary or supremely ugly. We say to ourselves, "Isn't So-and-so charming," or alternatively, "How positively plain is So-and-so."

As a matter of fact, the degree of beauty expressed in an individual's face ought to count for very little. What ought to count is the character which his or her features reveal. Let it be said quite definitely that faces indicate character more accurately than any other physical property of an individual. A person can change his voice and he can check his actions, but he cannot alter his features for more than a second at a time, and then only superficially.

Thus it comes about that faces are definite indications of character, and these indications are fairly easy to read, once the rules are learned. Of course, all such things as accidental blemishes, such as scars and broken noses, must be ignored at the outset.

First, let us take the general shape of the face.

THE SHAPE OF THE FACE.—There can be thousands of different shapes, but the normal is shown by Fig. 1, where the width across the forehead is more than across the chin. The forehead, the nose and the rest of the face should be about equal in length.

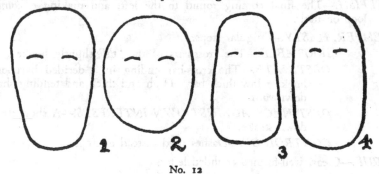

No. 12

Add to the width across the forehead and you have a brainy person, a clear thinker, a person whose opinions are worth considering. Of course, an excess of width in this place suggests some mental instability.

Fig. 2 shows an entirely different type. It may belong to a jolly person

40

who is excellent company; but do not go to him for sound advice. There is not enough length of forehead, nor width of forehead, to house a super-abundance of brains.

Fig. 3 introduces us to a ponderous type, slow-thinking, fond of food, and with animal instincts lurking in the background of his make-up.

Fig. 4 reveals a long face, narrow for its width. This belongs to a person who is limited in vision, and who can be very awkward at times. Such an individual will find it very hard to agree with others, especially in business matters. He may be deep and more often than not, he is a rather sad companion.

THE NOSE.—Fig. 1 shows the normal nose, betokening an average character.

Fig. 2 is too rounded at the tip. Force of character is lacking.

Fig. 3 reveals a drooping line between the tip of the nose and the upper lip. This stands for a character that loves amusements and is apt to neglect the real things of life.

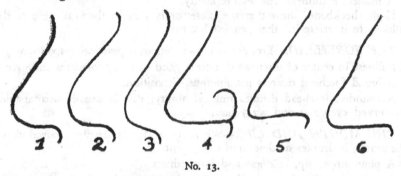

No. 13.

Fig. 4 gives a pronounced, fleshy curl where the nose joins the face. This is a sign that the possessor is a clear thinker, a leader of others, an intelligent person.

Fig. 5 shows a thin, pointed nose. The possessor is, probably, of a refined nature, but he or she is apt to be lacking in sympathy, even cruel.

Fig. 6 depicts a curved ridge. This is the nose of a person who lacks a refined nature. He may be jolly and humorous, but certainly not actuated by the highest ideals. Many noses of this shape are the result of an accident, which, of course, does not count.

A long nose indicates cautiousness, watchfulness, and often timidity.

A prominent nose that stands well out from the face shows a desire to observe and examine things, without the interference of others.

A fleshy tip to the nose displays a kindly nature, and a love of ease.

A short, small nose tells of conceit and a lack of sympathy for others.

A turned-up nose means that the possessor is a busybody, one who cannot keep a secret, but may be kind and generous.

THE EYES.—Large eyes denote love of talking and the ability to learn languages.

Small eyes denote secrecy and close-mindedness.

Full, dark eyes denote love of the opposite sex.

Truthful eyes are set straight in the head.

Untruthful eyes slope towards the nose.

Eyes that slope downwards from the nose are cruel and deceitful.

Eyes set widely apart denote breadth of mind.

Eyes set close together denote narrow-mindedness.

THE CHEEKS.—Full, rounded cheeks denote sociability and a love of friends.

Thin cheeks denote those who prefer their own company.

Fullness in lower part of cheek denotes love of eating and drinking.

A moderate fullness denotes hospitality.

High cheekbones show that the possessor is very methodical. He or she is likely to interfere in other people's business.

THE FOREHEAD.—Prominent brows denote a practical disposition.

Fullness in center of forehead denotes a good memory for dates and events.

A broad forehead denotes a humorous disposition.

A rounded forehead denotes musical ability; this is usually accompanied by curved eyebrows and wavy hair.

THE MOUTH AND LIPS.—When upper lip is deeply grooved down the center, it denotes modesty and refinement.

A plain upper lip, boldness and forwardness.

A long upper lip denotes self-esteem and self-control.

Redness and fullness in center of lip, love and passion for opposite sex.

Fullness at either side shows love of children and animals.

A mouth that displays the teeth when smiling denotes love of approbation and attention.

A full, red, well-developed lower lip denotes a kindly, sympathetic disposition.

Thin lips denote a hard, selfish, and unsympathetic nature. The same with straight lips.

THE CHIN.—A receding chin, as shown in Fig. 1, p. 43, denotes a lack of firmness. It belongs to a person who has insufficient will of his own.

A chin shaped as Fig. 2 or 3, or midway between these, provides a very acceptable character. There is determination and grit, without an excess of these qualities. Fig. 2 may be taken as the normal type.

Broad, bony structures of the chin denotes conscientiousness and straight-forwardness.

Length and projection of chin denotes firmness, stability, and perseverance.

An extremely long and projecting chin denotes stubbornness and ob-stinacy. (Fig. 4.)

A full ridge of fat under the chin denotes economy.

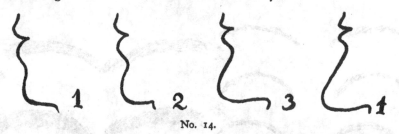

No. 14.

WRINKLES.—A wrinkle commencing in the lower cheek and extending right under the chin, from side to side, is caused from constant talking.

A wrinkle running from the side of the nose, downwards upon the lower cheek, to the outer corners of the mouth, is a sign of love of approbation.

Whenever in laughter three parallel circular lines are formed in the cheeks there is a fund of folly in the character.

Wrinkles lying horizontally across the root of the nose denote ability to command.

Several perpendicular wrinkles between the eyebrows denote a plodding, persevering disposition.

DIMPLES.—A round dimple in the chin denotes love of the beautiful in the opposite sex.

Dimples at the outer corners of the mouth are another sign of mirthfulness.

Dimples in the center of cheeks are another sign of approbation.

When a little cleft is seen at the tip of the nose it denotes the natural critic.

Close attention should always be given to texture and quality of the hair, eyes, and skin; this is most important, as the coarseness or refinement of character is shown very plainly to those who take the trouble to notice these things.

Color of hair, eyes, and skin is also very important; the depth of the feelings and passions is shown here; poorly colored people are much less passionate than their deeper colored fellow-creatures.

Thus from dark individuals of coarse quality we expect coarse passions, and from dark fine-quality individuals deep, refined emotions.

THE EYEBROWS.—Fig. 2 is intended for the eyebrows of a normal individual. Such a person goes about his duties in an ordinary, intelligent manner and does his best to make the world a little better place for having him in it.

In Fig. 1, the eyebrows have insufficient shape. They belong to an individual of extremes; he or she is either too determined or devoid of kindness.

In Fig. 3, the eyebrows are too curved, forming a full semi-circle. This is a sign of shallowness; they belong to a person who is not going to put himself out for somebody else.

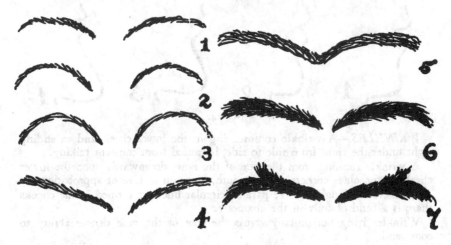

No. 15.

In Fig. 4, the eyebrows are higher at the outer than at the inner ends. Such are difficult to diagnose. They may belong to a very jolly, funny person; but they may also belong to someone absolutely untrustworthy, a foxy individual, in fact. They should be read in company with other facial signs.

In Fig. 5, the eyebrows meet on the nose. Hesitate before trusting a person so provided. He may be perfectly reliable, but make sure first.

Nos. 1 to 5 show eyebrows of fine or medium thickness, but Figs. 6 and 7 are coarser and heavier. Those that are neither too fine or too thick are best, since they are more likely to belong to a well-balanced person. Fine pencil streaks show a finniky, perhaps unkind nature. Heavy, bushy eyebrows point to an austere, querulous nature.

In Fig. 7, the upstanding hairs suggest a nature that may derive pleasure from posing.

A FINAL HINT.—In checking the "points" of a face, it is often found that one feature may contradict another. This does not prove that the explanations given above are incorrect. It goes to show that the character of the individual is not definitely set in one direction. He may vary at times or he may have the aptitude for fighting against one characteristic in favor of another. The only sound plan is to assess the character by striking a balance of all the "points" at issue.

HAVE YOU A MOLE?

Many people do not like these little marks, but let them be comforted, for in olden times, according to the wise men of the day, great reliance was placed on them. Just what a mole means depends on where it is to be found. The following may describe a mole of your own:—

RIGHT EYE (above).—Wealth and a happy marriage.

LEFT EYE (above).—You have a great liking for the opposite sex and you will, thereby, gain much happiness.

TEMPLE.—As above.

NOSE.—You will succeed in business.

CHEEK.—You will be happy, but not be blessed with fame and fortune.

CHIN. Fortunate in your choice of friends.

EAR (either).—A contented nature.

ARMS.—A happy nature, but with something of the "don't care" spirit.

SHOULDERS.—Will face difficulties with fortitude.

HANDS.—A practical nature. Able to take care of yourself.

LEGS.—Strong willed.

NECK.—You have a great deal of patience.

WHAT DO YOUR BUMPS MEAN?

Just feel the shape of your own head, and then ask a friend to let you do the same thing to him or her. Most likely you will be very surprised at the difference between the two. You may have bumps in certain places while your friend has them in totally different parts.

The science of phrenology, which is the reading of bumps, has discovered that bumps in certain places point to certain characteristics; if you have them, you must have the characteristics, and, if you have not them, you cannot have those qualities. In fact, the reading of character through the medium of bumps is a very definite science, and it is a science that can be easily learned and applied by almost anyone. Of course, there is much to learn, but there is no need to know a great deal if you merely want to assess a person's character in general terms.

A chart is supplied on p. 47, and on it is marked out just enough to enable you to read a head with ease. Only certain areas are mapped out; the rest of the head may be the location of bumps, but it does not present the bumps which are likely to interest us just now.

The areas are as follows:—

1.—*Lying at the top of the head, in the center and coming a little way towards the forehead.* If this area is well developed, it shows that the individual has a benevolent nature. He is generous and kind; he will work for the good of others and not think only of himself.

If the area is over-developed, the individual will be inclined to favor others at the expense of his own safety; if it is under-developed, he will be cruel and selfish.

2.—*Situated above but a little behind the eye; usually the place is just covered by hair.* When this area is well developed, it shows that the individual possesses plenty of happiness and a store of wit and mirth. He is a pleasant person, smiles on adversity and is excellent company.

If the area is over-developed, the individual is one who can never be taken seriously, who pokes fun at everything; if it is under-developed, he is the type of person who is never known to smile.

3.—*In the middle of the head, where it curves down towards the back of the neck.* In cases where this area is well developed, the person is one who has strength of mind; he is firm in his actions; he cannot be persuaded against his own judgment; and he likes his own way.

If this area is over-developed, the person is obstinate and stubborn; if it is under-developed, he is easily led, apt to waver and has not a mind of his own.

46

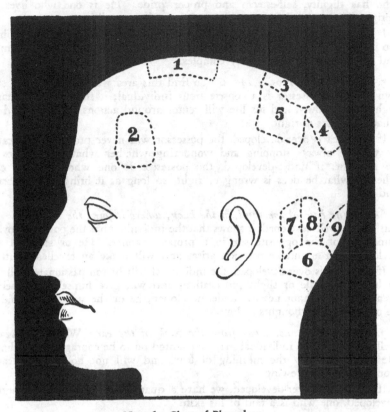

No. 16.—Chart of Phrenology.

1 — Benevolence, generosity, kindness.
2 — Happiness, Wit, Mirth.
3 — Firmness, Strength of Mind.
4 — Self-Esteem, Dignity, Pride.
5 — Conscientiousness, Sense of Duty.
6 — Love.
7 — Courage.
8 — Desire for Marriage.
9 — Love of Children.

4.—*In the middle of the head, lower down at the back than No. 3.* When this area is found in a well-developed condition, the possessor is a person who has dignity, self-esteem and proper pride. He is one who lives an upright life because he puts a high price on these qualities.

If this area is over-developed, the individual is over-confident, he thinks too much of himself and is haughty; if it lacks development, he is too humble and suffers from an inferiority complex.

5.—*Lying beside Nos. 3 and 4.* To find this area well developed is a sure sign that the possessor is a conscientious individual; it shows that he has a high sense of duty, and his life will center around actions that are based on what he thinks is right.

If this area is over-developed, the possessor will never progress far because he will be always stopping and wondering whether what he proposes to do is right; if under-developed, the possessor is one who does not care whether what he does is wrong or right, so long as it brings him pleasure and gain.

6.—*At the base of the skull, at the back, where it joins the backbone.* If this area is well developed, it shows that the individual has the power of loving somebody of the opposite sex in a proper manner. He or she will fall in love when a suitable occasion arises and will make an excellent partner.

If this area is over-developed, the individual will be too passionate, will fall in love with little or slight provocation, and will give himself or herself a great deal of unhappiness; if under-developed, he or she will be too cold to be moved by the thoughts of love.

7.—*A slight distance away from the back of the ear.* When this area is well developed, the individual may be counted on to be courageously inclined. He will not know the meaning of fear, and will not hold back because troubles may be brewing.

If this area is over-developed, we have a quarrelsome person and if under-developed, one who is afraid of his skin.

8.—*Beside No. 7, but more in the center of the back of the head.* Whenever this area is properly developed, it shows that the possessor would make an admirable husband or wife. He or she would be devoted, loyal and attentive.

If the area is over-developed, the possessor has a jealous disposition; if under-developed, he or she is fickle and apt to flirt with others.

9.—*Beside No. 8, in the center of the back of the head, low down.* Should this area be well developed, it shows that the possessor has a proper love and regard for children and that he thinks no person has experienced the fullest joys of life who has not become a parent.

If this area is over-developed, the possessor thinks so much of children that he spoils them; if it is under-developed, he is of the type that "cannot stand them at any price."

HOW ASTROLOGY DECIDES YOUR DESTINY

Astrology is one of the oldest sciences in the world. It is said to have originated with the Egyptians, almost at the very beginning of time. Indeed, it is almost impossible to trace a period when this science was not practiced.

There is nothing new under the sun, and its close followers will scarcely allow any errors in its deductions. They go so far as to declare it to be an exact science, a term which means that everything can be reasoned out and proved; nothing is left to guesswork.

Such sciences are Mathematics, Algebra, and Geometry. We need not believe that Astrology is all this, but certainly some very startling and accurate predictions have been made by astrologers.

However, as in all other methods of fortunetelling attempted by us mortals, it is far from infallible. So long as we do not take it to be exact and sure, we shall get plenty of amusement and interest from its study, with the exciting feeling all the time at the back of our minds that "it might come true."

Here is a list giving you the names and meanings given to planets by astrologers.

Name.	Approximate meaning given by Astrologers.
Mars.	Strength.
Venus.	Beauty.
Mercury.	Capacity for adapting oneself.
Uranus.	Improvement.
Sun.	Life.
Jupiter.	Freedom and growth.
Saturn.	Diminished—shrinking—lack of growth.
Neptune.	Able to receive—receptive.
Earth.	Physical—not spiritual.
The Moon.	Feeling.

The main idea at the back of astrology is that the planets (or starry bodies which revolve round the sun) each have a strong and varying influence upon the minds of human beings.

THE ZODIAC.—Of course when the planets revolve round the sun they travel through a course or path. The Zodiac is the name given by astronomers to the boundary which encloses this course or path in the sky.

The signs of the Zodiac are the spaces into which the Zodiac is divided.

Here are the signs of the Zodiac arranged in order to show which signs are opposite to each other.

	facing	
Aries.		Libra.
Taurus.		Scorpio.
Gemini.		Sagittarius.
Cancer.		Capricorn.
Leo.		Aquarius.
Virgo.		Pisces.

Now each sign has a planet which is said to rule it; this is called the ruling planet. It is from the nature of this planet that the probable character and fate of the individual are told. It is not necessary to know the whys and wherefores of this, if you have not studied astronomy it will only serve to muddle you, and if, on the other hand, you do understand astronomy you will not need any explanation. We will just say what does happen, and that will tell you all you need in these first steps.

Well, we all know that the earth revolves upon its axis once in every 24 hours. Now, according to astronomers, this causes one of the Zodiac signs to appear in the eastern sky, where it remains for two hours. We have said that each sign has a planet ruling it, so the sign that appears on the sky at the time of birth decides what planet that person is born under or is influenced by.

Let us suppose for a moment that you were born when the sign Libra was rising, as the saying is. The planet which rules Libra is Venus, so the person born at that time would be a Venus type, i.e., a person having the influence of Venus upon him.

In addition to the main, ruling planet, astrologers will tell you that there are other "neighboring" planets—we will call them neighboring because it is a simple term—which also have their effect upon us. Astrologers call this one planet being "in aspect" with another. For instance, you might have the planet Mars in aspect with (or influenced by) the planet Saturn; you would then be dealing with a very strong character.

The qualities of Mars which give the fighter and the pushing type, or in excess the bully, will be well steadied by the qualities of Saturn, which by themselves give coldness and, in excess, lack of feeling. The two together result in a character remarkable for its steadiness combined with its never-wearying energy and good balance.

So you see, we seldom find pure types (i.e., qualities of Mars, or other planets by themselves), and it is very fortunate that this is so; we should get a very one-sided world if we did.

Now we come to that part of Astrology which really interests most people; here will be shown the birth-dates for each month in the year and the probable characters of persons born at that special time. You may ask why the characters are given and why not the fate or future of the person concerned. The reason is this: you can be pretty sure that what you read of an individual's character will give you a sound idea of what in all probability his future will be.

After all, the carving out of our lives is in our own hands. We are the masters of our fate, or as the song has it, "Captain of our Soul."

However, if we believe astrologers, there is a way to tell the times of our lives when matters should go smoothly or the reverse. The most favorable times for speculating with money, starting in business, in fact, the most and least favorable periods of our lives can, according to astrology, be worked out by what is known as the Horoscope.

Now this Horoscope is in reality a chart of your life. The rocky waters are shown, and the barrier reefs which each of us must avoid through our life, so you will see a use in the study of astrology. It would seem to be Nature's warning to us all of the necessity for effort, effort and again effort.

Here are the birth dates and characteristics of persons born between the dates mentioned. Since astrology is not infallible, do not take all these characteristics too seriously.

You will notice that each date is taken from about the 20th of one month to the 20th of the next month.

WHEN WERE YOU BORN?

Dec. 22nd to Jan. 20th.

People born during this period have considerable mental ability and a keen business instinct. They are fond of the imaginative arts. They are proud; they like their own way and they see that they get it. Generally speaking, they are better fitted to lead than to follow others.

However, they do not take kindly to changes of any kind, and are annoyed by newfangled ideas. They do not want the advice of other people and often resent it. They do not strike out in new directions and they avoid taking risks. They lack "push."

To these people, we say:

Don't wait for opportunities—make them.

Don't let your pride persuade you to keep on the wrong road rather than turn back.

Don't be afraid of admitting and correcting a mistake.

Don't run away from trouble; meet it with a bold front.

Jan. 21st to Feb. 19th.

People born during this period have a strong sense of duty. They have a kindly disposition and are inclined to be affectionate. They refuse to think ill of anyone until the bad qualities are proved. Being straightforward themselves, they imagine everyone else is the same and, on this account, they are likely to suffer some bitter experiences.

However, they lack a proper regard for their own welfare. They are a little too confiding and they are not adaptable. Once they make up their minds on a matter, it is almost impossible to persuade them to change it.

To these people we say:

Don't brood over troubles. Face the facts, fight them out, and then, forget all about them.

Don't be guided by impulses.

Don't neglect the financial side of things, if you want to succeed.

Feb. 20th to March 20th.

People born during this period are just in their dealings, and would not injure another willingly. Their code of honor is a strict one. They are industrious and persistent. They endeavor to perform their share in making the world a better and a happier place.

However, they are too cautious and do not take sufficient risks to make life a complete success. Too often, they ask themselves whether they should go ahead with a project and, while they are hesitating, the opportune moment flies away.

To these people, we say:

Don't listen to the voice of despair.

Don't be downhearted, if you don't see, at first, the way to do a thing.

Don't think in small things. Think large.

March 21st to April 19th.

People born during this period are thoughtful. They are artistic, are fond of the fine arts, and like all that is beautiful. They are self-willed and rebel when others try to drive them. They do not take much notice of convention, and the way of the world means nothing to them.

However, they are apt to shrink from disagreeable work, and everything sordid disgusts them. They are too sensitive and take offense too readily.

To these people, we say:

Don't set yourself against the world: you will lose if you do.

Don't tire of your task before it is done.

Don't be too thin-skinned.

Don't forget that it takes all sorts of people to make up the world.

April 20th to May 20th.

People born during this period possess a warm and generous heart. They are good workers and display a genuine interest in everything they undertake. They possess the kind of mind that seems to act instinctively and which does not depend so much on real reason. They are lavish in gifts and kindness.

However, they are liable to rush to extremes, and they lack balance. Consequently, they are easily misled.

To these people, we say:

Don't get excited unnecessarily.

Don't be too easily persuaded.

Don't allow your emotions to master you.

May 21st to June 21st.

People born during this period are ambitious and they aspire to very high things. They are sensitive and sympathetic. They have lively imaginations and they are given to building castles in the air. They are naturally eloquent and are never at a loss for something to say.

However, they are rarely content with things as they find them. Consequently, they grumble a great deal. They do not weigh up the "pros and cons" before deciding on a matter; and they jump to conclusions.

To these people, we say:

Don't be discouraged too quickly.

Dream if you like, but don't neglect to translate your dreams into realities.

Don't be too enthusiastic.

Don't forget that work rather than plans win a home.

June 22nd to July 22nd.

People born during this period are highly generous and they make sacrifices in order to help others. They do nothing in a half-hearted way, whether it is work or play. They are persevering and the home is put before anything else.

However, they dislike changes which mean an alteration in domestic life and they are a trifle old-fashioned in some of their beliefs. A little flattery or persuasion is apt to lead them astray, and their better judgment is rapidly overborne by a strong personality.

To these people, we say:

Don't dash headlong into anything.

Don't be irritable under contradiction.

Don't let your emotions run away with you.

Don't spoil your chances for a little show of love.

July 23rd to August 21st.

People born during this period easily adapt themselves to circumstances, and they are considered "jolly good company." They have "push" and enterprise in a marked degree. They are affectionate, generous and highly capable.

However, they lack a certain amount of self-control and they are not always dependable. They frequently forget promises, and they are often late in keeping appointments. In money affairs, they are likely to overlook their obligations.

To these people, we say:

Don't let your emotions sweep you off your feet.

Don't become downcast too easily.

Don't be obstinate.

Don't make up your mind in a hurry.

August 22nd to Sept. 22nd

People born during this month are well equipped for the battle of life, and they have several qualities which should bring them success. They are not easily flurried, and they know how to stand firm in an emergency. They are quick in perceiving the correct thing to do, no matter what it is. They are capable, dependable and thorough.

However, they are prone to be too independent, and they are apt to disregard good advice, preferring their own judgment. They are not quick in making friends because they are too wrapped up in themselves.

To these people, we say:

Don't take a plunge before reckoning up everything first.

Don't forget that there are two sides to every question. There is yours and the other man's.

Don't fall into the habit of doing tomorrow what should be done today.

Sept. 23rd to Oct. 23rd.

People born during this month are far-seeing and have excellent judgment. They have a passion for "finding out" things, and they want to know about everything that happens. Consequently, they are intelligent. They make delightful companions.

However, they are bad losers, and they often let themselves get out of hand. This seriously hurts their vanity, as they are exceedingly desirous of creating a good impression.

To these people, we say:

Don't speak until you have thought twice.

Don't be obstinate. Admit you are wrong when you know you are.

Don't abuse your opponent.

Oct. 24th to Nov. 22nd.

People born during this month possess great ambition, and are persevering. They are full of energy and passionate spirit. One rebuff does not stop them; they return to the fray again and again, until they have conquered. They are precise in their actions, neat, methodical and tidy.

However, they are domineering, and endeavor to impose their will on others. They lack discrimination and, once they conceive a hatred, there is nothing which can dispel it.

To these people, we say:

Don't domineer.

Don't do things when you feel resentful.

Don't forget that prim and proper things sometimes defeat their own ends.

Nov. 23rd to Dec. 21st.

People born during this month are, usually, virile and full of go and enterprise. They have more will power than the average and know how to surmount obstacles. Nothing comes amiss to them, and they are self-reliant.

However, they are inclined to quarrel with those who offer advice. They carry independence too far, and they often speak without realizing the significance of their words. They seldom confide in others.

To these people, we say:

Don't act or speak and then think. Think first.

Don't be obstinate and think you are being determined.

Don't be headstrong and disregard advice that is disinterested.

Don't be carried away by fickle fancies.

YOUR CHILD'S OCCUPATION DECIDED
BY THE STARS

It is a well-known fact that every human being is considerably influenced, as far as character and capabilities are concerned, by the time of the year in which he or she was born. That being so, it follows that the occupation best suited to any particular individual is, in a measure, related to his or her birth-date.

Parents who are anxious to do the best for their children should take note of these conditions; they may be helpful in keeping round pegs out of square holes. Below, we offer suggestions which have proved of use in thousands of cases, where doubt had previously existed. The information may be used in this way: Suppose a child is about to leave school and is ready to make his or her entry into the world of work. In a number of cases, the child has a very definite idea of what he or she wants to do. If the work is reasonably suited to the child's temperament, station in life, and so on, it is much the best plan to allow him or her to follow the particular bent. It is just as well to note whether the chosen occupation fits in with the work which we list below for his or her individual birth-date. If it approximates to some occupation which we mention, well and good. Let the child go ahead, there is every chance of success. But, if it is quite alien to anything which is given in the list, caution is needed. We do not say that the child's ambition should be checked and that he or she should be put to a job of our selection, but we do say that caution ought to be exercised. We are perfectly ready to admit that the stars and the birth-date are not the only factors which count. Environment, upbringing, the father's occupation, and other things must influence the child. All these influences should be weighed and carefully considered.

But where astrology and the stars can give most help is in the case of a boy or girl who has no formulated idea as to what he or she wants to become. Thousands of children reach the school-leaving age without showing the slightest inkling for any particular job. To the parents of such children, we say, consult the lists set out below, seeing that they are based on astrological teachings. Go over the selected occupations carefully, discuss them with the child, explain what they offer in terms of money, work, hours, etc., and watch the effect they have on the child. In this way, it will soon be possible to gain an idea as to what occupation should be eventually decided on.

Here are the occupations suitable for each person:

CAPRICORN BORN (Dec. 22nd to Jan. 20th).—Since people born in this period have considerable mental ability, it follows that they do well in most of the professions, since they can pass the necessary examinations and become well qualified. Thus, they ought to do satisfactorily in medicine, the law, dentistry, the scholastic profession and similar occupations. The fact that they do not care to take risks unfits them for many business openings, but where aspirations are not high, they do well as clerks and in filling posts which consist of routine work. Girls, especially, should seek work which is connected with the imaginative arts.

AQUARIAN BORN (Jan. 21st to Feb. 19th).—Boys display a good deal of interest in occupations which require the use of their hands. This makes them capable in many engineering posts, in wireless, in cabinet-making and similar jobs. They are not good at creating or inventing in connection with these industries, however. There is the roving disposition implanted in these boys and many of them think that the pilot's job on an air liner could not be equalled.

Girls are, also, interested in working with their hands: thus they are fitted for dressmaking, the millinery trade, for dealing with arts and crafts supplies, etc. A certain number are eminently suited to secretarial work.

PISCEAN BORN (Feb. 20th to March 20th).—Children born in this period have a love for the sea and, therefore, the boys find congenial work as ship's mates, stewards, marine engineers, etc., while girls are suitable for stewardesses and other jobs filled by women on ocean-going vessels.

In addition boys and girls are both fitted to all kinds of work in shops, chain stores, etc., but they are not at their best when managing their own businesses. They require authority behind them.

A few Pisceans have artistic ability which should lead them to do splendidly as authors, painters, musicians, etc.

ARIES BORN (March 21st to April 19th).—The Aries child is often a problem, for certain of them have a rooted objection to anything in the nature of routine work. They chafe at going and coming at the same hour each day, and of doing the same work year after year. It is not that they are lazy, but that their nature refuses to be driven by set rules. With such children, it is wisest to interest them in whatever they fancy, until the time comes when they launch out on some brilliant scheme of their own. Aries men are the ones that fill unusual, out-of-the-way posts.

Where this rooted objection does not exist, the children are good in almost any position which permits of movement, as travellers, for instance.

TAURIAN BORN (April 20th to May 20th).—As a rule, children who are Taurians are very successful. They do not mind hard work and they have a "flair" for doing the right thing, without knowing why. They have a head for figures and money, and thus do well in banks and stockbroker's offices. They take kindly to long training, which enables them to succeed in law and medicine.

Both boys and girls are good with their hands. This makes them successful in a large number of occupations, as widely diverse as engineering and tailoring, or hairdressing and piano playing.

GEMINI BORN (May 21st to June 21st).—Gemini children show a good deal of ambition, and their chief fault is that they object to beginning at the bottom of the ladder. Perhaps this is useful, in a way, as it goads them on to climbing upwards. They have a good deal of vision. Thus they make excellent newspaper men and women. They do well in new trades, notably in radio and the motor world. Also, they ought to make a success in certain branches of aviation. Their eloquence fits them admirably for travellers, and they would make their mark in any business which, eventually, gave them work of an imaginative nature. In a general way, they find interest in theatrical work, in literary activities and in architecture. All Gemini people have a streak in their natures which causes them to seek unnecessary changes.

CANCER BORN (June 22nd to July 22nd).—Children born during this preiod are usually "workers." They will plod, they do not mind long hours, and they will set themselves to difficult jobs, if told to get on with them. As a rule, they should be set to something which enables them to work "on their own." They much prefer this to being a small peg in a large machine. They are suited to small businesses and agencies. A mail-order business might fit in with their requirements. Girls would do well as private teachers, running small schools of their own. They are, also, suited to the drapery trade.

LEO BORN (July 23rd to August 21st).—Those who are born during this period succeed best in what might be called "clean" occupations. The boys do not want to put on overalls and become grimy, and the girls prefer work that enables them to be always neat and tidy. Both of them show aptitude in marketing such things as jewelry, drugs, books and clothes, but they do not want to be concerned with making them. They are not so much interested in vending the necessaries of life as the luxuries. Thus, motor cars, victrolas, cameras, sports requisites, etc., attract them.

They are not much suited to clerical work, but a good number find an outlet for their ambitions in the theatrical and literary world, while a few make good dentists, radiologists and medical practitioners.

VIRGO BORN (Aug. 22nd to Sept. 22nd).—These children are capable, but their great failing is that, once they find a fairly suitable post, they will not look for anything better. They prefer to hold on to a moderate certainty than to risk a little for a great success. Consequently, Virgo-born are found living on salaries just sufficient to keep them from want.

They are eminently suited to clerical work of the higher types, such as in banks, insurance companies, stockbrokers' offices, etc. They make good company secretaries, excellent journalists, fairly good actors and actresses, and the girls do well as teachers.

LIBRA BORN (Sept. 23rd to October 23rd).—Children of this period do not mind hard work, but they hate monotony, especially if it is at all sordid. They have good judgment, a quality which fits them for such diverse occupations as medicine and the drama, the law and dressmaking. No special trades or professions can be singled out for them; but, as long as they are set to work in a direction which provides them with an outlet for a nicely balanced judgment and a capacity for what might be termed the detective instinct, they should succeed admirably.

SCORPIO BORN (Oct. 24th to Nov. 22nd).—There is an abundance of ambition in these children, and they seek position rather than money. Thus, the boys do well in the Navy and the Army, and, in a less degree, in the Air Force. The Church holds out good openings for many of them, and the Mercantile Marine interest not a few. Medicine attracts both boys and girls, and so does the stage. Anything to do with chemicals seems to influence many of the boys. Scorpio-born children are often heard to say that they want to make a name for themselves.

SAGITTARIAN BORN (Nov. 23rd to Dec. 21st).—Children of this period are fond of animals; thus they are suited to become veterinary surgeons, horse-dealers, farmers and even jockeys. One section of them, having excessive will power and plenty of self-reliance, makes a type of individual who seeks publicity in the political world. All are capable in business, especially in the executive branches. Not a few men become company promoters, chairmen and directors. The girls make excellent teachers and welfare workers.

WHAT ARE YOUR HOBBIES?

According to your Zodiac sign you have a disposition for certain hobbies. You may not necessarily have these hobbies but your inclinations lie towards them.

CAPRICORN BORN.—Gardening. Nature Study. Rambles in the countryside. Making things of almost any kind. Chemistry. Physics.

AQUARIAN BORN.—Aviation, ranging from actual flying to making aeroplane models. Gliding. Constructing all kinds of articles. Painting pictures. Drawing. Needlework.

PISCES BORN.—Traveling, especially by sea. Photography. Constructing and using wireless apparatus. Making electrical apparatus. Theater-going and amateur theatricals. Arts and crafts (girls).

ARIES BORN.—Traveling, touring. Anything connected with motor cars. Sight-seeing. Making things. Reading. Arts and crafts (girls).

TAURUS BORN.—Constructive hobbies, from wireless to the building of houses. Walking. Golf. Swimming. Collecting antiques.

GEMINI BORN.—Likely to be interested in inventions. Good at solving puzzles. Football. Tennis. Nature rambling. Girls have a bent for household duties, such as cooking, needlework, etc.

CANCER BORN.—Interested in the wonders of the world. Anxious to see things and people. Music. Reading. Collecting antiques. Almost any outdoor game. Girls are fond of needlework of the finer kinds.

LEO BORN.—Hobbies allied to the daily work. Intellectual reading, especially anything bearing on historical matters. Going about. Golf. Swimming. Making things of an artistic nature.

VIRGO BORN.—Indoor games. Making and repairing household articles. Good at manual activities, from playing the piano to constructing toys. Prefers to be amused indoors than out in the open.

LIBRA BORN.—Doing things to keep the home ship-shape. Football. Cricket. Photography. Reading. Wireless. Needlework and knitting (girls).

SCORPIO BORN.—Scientific recreations of all kinds. Keeping pets. Nature rambling. Girls take a keen interest in household duties. Card playing. Seeing people. Dabbling in mysterious matters, such as thought-reading, table-rapping, seances, etc.

SAGITTARIAN BORN.—Hobbies of an intellectual character. Walking. Outdoor sports. Boxing. Nature study. Keeping pets. Reading.

59

WHAT IS YOUR LUCKY NUMBER?

Once more from the rising sun of the East further marvelous theories have reached us through the paths of the ages. To many of our prosaic Western minds, maybe not unnaturally, these ideas will at first sight appear almost ridiculous. However, do not condemn numerical mysteries unheard, for no Manual of Fortunetelling would be complete should it not include a talk on this most arresting subject.

Students of numbers, as do astrologers and students of palmistry, declare that there is no such thing as luck or chance in the world. They also state that we are strongly but not inevitably influenced by certain powerful laws of Nature.

Number science is certainly unknown to the great majority of us, but there are some superstitions which are based on evil numbers; these superstitions we treat with great respect. Very few of us really care to sit down thirteen at table, while I have known a man go sad and smokeless rather than be the third to light his cigarette off one match!

Fortunetelling by numbers is allied to astrology very closely indeed. Let us now take each day of the week individually and see what information we can get from it. You will find that very useful as a check upon your other forms of fortunetelling.

ON WHAT DAY WERE YOU BORN?

If, as I suggested, we take the days of the week we shall find that they in turn are influenced by the order in which they are found, or by the number which is theirs. For instance, Sunday being the first day, is influenced by No. 1, and Friday, being the sixth day takes No. 6 as its ruling number.

According to the ancients each number has its corresponding planet; here is a little table showing the planet representing and ruling over each number.

No. 0. Represented by Space.
No. 1. Represented by The Sun.
No. 2. Represented by The Moon.
No. 3. Represented by Mars.
No. 4. Represented by Mercury.

No. 5. Represented by Jupiter.
No. 6. Represented by Venus.
No. 7. Represented by Saturn.
No. 8. Represented by Uranus.
No. 9. Represented by Neptune.

Taking each day of the week in order, we find the following characteristics.

TABLE OF DAYS IN WEEK

No. 1 *(Sunday)*.—You will see by your table that this day takes the Sun for its ruler—Sun-day. It is a fortunate day; persons born on a Sunday have a brave and honest influence on them. They will be optimistic, but not foolishly so, while at the same time they have great pride in the reputation of themselves and their families. If they have any fault it is, maybe, that this pride is felt, a little too strongly; they may be inclined to take themselves rather too seriously. However, I repeat, this is an excellent day.

No. 2 *(Monday)*.—This day is the Moon-day. The lesson for Monday men to learn is steadiness. They are too easily influenced and are blown hither and thither upon life's winds. They adapt themselves well to change of place, circumstances, scene, and frequently follow the sea. They have plenty of imagination in their natures, and should cultivate common sense.

No. 3 *(Tuesday)*.—The day of Mars (French—Mardi). Frequently the engineers of the world. An ambitious go-ahead day is Tuesday. These Tuesday folk are the explorers, the men who emigrate, and the earnest patriots of life. Soldiers, workers at the furnace among other workers, are found among those born on Tuesday. Their womenfolk are inclined to be rather shrewish and domineering. They are not naturally good managers, and should cultivate this quality because they are always rare workers.

No. 4 *(Wednesday)*.—The table tells us that these are the Mercurians. The men are quick at calculating figures, and always capable and thoughtful workers. Mercury, as its name implies, gives quickness, with business trading capacity. The women appear not to be so favorably influenced, they must guard against grumbling and gossip; then they may do well enough.

No. 5 *(Thursday)*.—Under the planet of Jupiter, these Thursday people have many good qualities. They are liberal and good natured, but have one vice—the outcome of their virtue. They are inclined to be too liberal with themselves, which is extravagance. Given an idea they can turn it to good account, but do not, as a rule, originate ideas. Statesmen are here found; let these Jupiterians beware of a love of display and what is commonly known as side. Then they are very excellent people indeed.

No. 6 *(Friday)*.—Look at the table—see Venus is the planet of Friday. This accounts for many things. Here we see the typical Venus type. Gay, light-hearted, with no thought of the morrow, they flit happily through life like a gilded butterfly upon the wing. If they lack taste they over-dress. Their good qualities are their charming personalities, pleasing manners, and a quick command of music and art. They should beware of being only butterflies, and should cultivate strength of character. They should also obtain by hook or by crook a liking for hard work; it will serve them in good stead.

No. 7 *(Saturday)*.—Saturday, as its name tells us, has sad Saturn for its planet. Here we have the exact opposite to the persons mentioned who were born on a Friday. Saturday people miss half the joy of living by their cold and calculating natures. Careful with money, they are patient workers, they must beware of being miserly, and should certainly cultivate their missing sense of humor. The good qualities in these people are their sincerely earnest outlook and their capacity for an almost endless grind of

hard work. Their womenfolk frequently make old maids and should practice sweet temper and a kindly feeling towards the rest of the household.

YOUR OWN NUMBER

But there is much more in the science of numbers than that which can
be gleaned from the days of the week. There is your own personal number,
the number which influences you and your actions more than any other.
If you know your number, think how you can use it for good and avoid
others for ill! The finding of your number is a simple matter when you
have mastered the elements of numerology, which is the science of numbers.

Let us explain how your own number is found. First, write down your
birth-date, the day of the month, the month itself and the year. Thus, three
items are required. Take first the day of the month. If it consists of one
figure, leave it. If it consists of two, add them together, and, if the answer
comes to two figures, add them together. All this may appear a little involved, but it is not, as one or two examples will show.

Suppose you were born on the 9th of the month, then 9 is the number
you want.

But, suppose it was the 16th, then six and one make seven. Therefore
7 is the required number.

Again, if you were born on the 29th, then nine and two make eleven, but
as eleven consists of two figures, you must add them together, and they
make 2.

So much for the day of the month, now for the month itself. January
stands for one, February for 2, and so on, to December for 12. The numbers
of the months from January to September can stand as they are, but October
November and December, being 10, 11 and 12, must be added up, as already
described. Thus October is one, November is two and December three.

Thirdly, the number of the year must be considered. Say you were born
in 1910. These figures add up to eleven, and eleven, being double figures,
adds up to 2. Therefore 1910 is equivalent to 2.

Work out your figures here.

You have now obtained three separate figures, add them together and if
they come to a one-figure number, that is the number which you require.
On the other hand, if it is a double-figured amount, add the two figures
as before, until you arrive at a single-figured amount. Then that is the
number you require.

So as to make the whole thing perfectly clear, we will take a complete
example and work it out, exactly as you must work out your own birth-date.

Example.—12th September, 1913.

$$12 = 1 + 2 = 3$$
September is the 9th month $= 9$
$$1913 = 1 + 9 + 1 + 3 = 14 = 1 + 4 = 5$$
$$3 + 9 + 5 = 17 = 1 + 7 = 8$$

Therefore, the personal number of anyone born on 12th September, 1913, is 8. Eight should guide and influence all his or her actions. We are not going to pretend that benefits will accrue on every occasion that the personal number is observed, but we are going to say that we have noted some marvelous pieces of good fortune when it has.

When you have found your personal number, there are several ways in which you can use it. Suppose your number is the one just found, eight; then you can conclude that the eighth day of any month will be a propitious one for you. But that is not the only one. The 17th is equally good, because one plus seven gives eight. Moreover, the 26th is in a similar position. Two and six make eight.

Yet another way to use your personal number arises when you want to know whether some important step should be taken on a definite day. What is the particular day? Add up its numerological values, exactly as you did with your birthday, and if it resolves itself into the same number as your personal number, you may go ahead with cheerfulness. Put forth your best effort, and, on the day, you will have ample chances of success.

THE NUMBER OF YOUR NAME

Numerology permits of still another step. Take your own name and see what number it is equal to. You will be able to do this in the following way: A stands for one, B for two, C for three, and so on. When you reach I, which is 9, commence again and give J the value of one, then continue. To make all this clear, we will set out the values of the complete alphabet:

1 =	A	J	S	6 =	F	O	X
2 =	B	K	T	7 =	G	P	Y
3 =	C	L	U	8 =	H	Q	Z
4 =	D	M	V	9 =	I	R	—
5 =	E	N	W				

Thus, suppose your name is Joan Shirley, the letters resolve themselves into the following numbers:—

$$J \quad O \quad A \quad N \quad S \quad H \quad I \quad R \quad L \quad E \quad Y$$
$$1 + 6 + 1 + 5 + 1 + 8 + 9 + 9 + 3 + 5 + 7 = 55$$
$$55 = 5 + 5 = 10 = 1 + 0 = 1$$

From all that we have said, it will be clear that the birthdate may be used for finding the personal number, or the letters of the name may be used. On rare occasions, the two ways will provide the same number. When this is the case, great faith should be placed in that number. But, when the two ways give different numbers, what? Does one disprove the other? No. You simply have two numbers favorable to you. The birthdate number is the more definite and reliable because your very existence is based on it.

A word at the end. Married ladies must use their maiden name for finding the name number.

DO YOU KNOW THAT

Odd Numbers have always been credited with mystic powers capable of influencing the destinies of people; and a curious survival of the idea is to be found in the fact that countrywomen, without knowing why, put an odd number of eggs under their hens in the belief that otherwise no chickens will be hatched?

In addition, we have noticed that books of sweepstake tickets generally have the odd-numbered tickets withdrawn from them before the even-numbered ones.

Number Three.—This number comes in for a considerable share of popularity, even from mythological times, when there were the three fates and the three graces. Shakespeare introduced three witches in "Macbeth." In nursery rhymes, we have the three blind mice. In public-house signs, we frequently come across the numeral "three," and, of course, pawnbrokers have three brass balls.

Number Seven.—Seven is deemed extremely lucky, it being the perfect or mystic number which runs the entire scheme of the Universe in matters physical and spiritual. Man's life is popularly divided into seven ages: the product of seven and nine—sixty-three—was regarded as the grand climacteric, and the age was considered as a most important stage of life.

The seventh son of a seventh son, according to Highland belief, possesses the gift of second sight, and the power of healing the sick. Many people believe that a cycle of seven years of misfortune is likely to be succeeded by another of prosperity.

Number Nine is credited with mystic properties, good and bad. A piece of wool with nine knots tied in it is a well-known charm for a sprained ankle. The cat o'nine tails is a form of punishment not to be taken lightly.

Number Thirteen.—Of this number, everybody can supply instances when it has brought bad luck. But it may be cheering to mention that, in certain parts of the world, thirteen is regarded in quite a favorable light. Whether it is good or bad is a matter for each individual to decide.

YOUR LUCKY COLOR

The old saying, "green for grief," is a well-known one, and the writer would rather wear any color on earth than green, not even a green scarf or belt. Moreover, she sees to it that the other members of the family do not indulge in the unlucky color. But mind you, green only brings her ill-fortune when used for wearing apparel. There is no objection, of course, to a green front-door nor to wallpaper of the same color. For such uses, green plays its part harmlessly enough.

Though green dresses are more distressing to the writer than a red rag to a bull, she is quite prepared to admit that many people find it a very lucky color. This brings us to the point. There is no color that is universally unlucky; it is only so in the hands of certain individuals. With others, it may be an absolute harbinger of all that is lucky. Even green may do this.

Now the question is, "Which is your lucky color?" If you know it, well and good. Make use of it in every possible way. When wearing dresses made of it, you will feel more confident of yourself than when arrayed in something else. You will get more work done, and it will be better work. The only thing is that you must be sure that it is your lucky color. If you are not quite sure, the tonic effect is absolutely lost.

Not only should you wear your fortunate color, but it is a good plan to surround yourself with it. We know a woman who pins her faith to purple. Her dresses are mostly purple; the wallpaper in her bedroom is purple; purple casement curtains adorn the windows; there are purple rugs in various parts of the house; even the back of the hair-brush on her dressing table is purple. And, since she decided that purple was her lucky color and used it in every reasonable way, she has had several strokes of marvelous good fortune.

But, of course, you may say in reply to all this that you do not know your lucky color. What then? This is where we can give you a little help. Most people's lucky color depends on the time of their birth and the following list sets out the birth colors. We know full well that everybody does not derive good fortune from his birth color, but that they find it in some other hue. Therefore, the proper course is to make trials with the appropriate color listed below and, if that does not answer satisfactorily, to choose another of your own liking and try that. Only by personal experiment can you finally decide the point.

These are the birth-colors. The first given for any period is the one almost universally accepted. Those following after the first are, however, favored by a certain number of people.

65

Birth Date	Colors
Dec. 22nd to Jan. 20th	Emerald Green Sapphire Blue Black
Jan. 21st to Feb. 19th	Various Blues Dark Green
Feb. 20th to March 20th	Purple White Silver
March 21st to April 19th	Rose Red
April 20th to May 20th	Turquoise Blue Other shades of Blue
May 21st to June 21st	Light shades of Yellow Orange Gold
June 22nd to July 22nd	Mauve White Silver
July 23rd to August 21st	Gold Brown Yellow
Aug. 22nd to Sept. 22nd	Yellow Orange Light Blue
Sept. 23rd to Oct. 23rd	Rose Pink Yellow
Oct. 24th to Nov. 22nd	Dark Green Red Brown
Nov. 23rd to Dec. 21st	Purple Blue

COLORS, of course, have certain values attached to them:
> White is a symbol of purity.
> Red is typical of fire, blood and anger.
> Orange stands for marriage.
> Green recalls spring and suggests youth and hope.
> Purple means royalty and everything regal.
> Yellow is associated with great success.
> Black is a symbol of sadness and mourning.

WHICH IS YOUR LUCKY STONE?

Ever since time began, it has been a common belief that people derived luck and good fortune by wearing precious stones. A stone, however, that brought luck to one person might be ineffective when worn by someone else. Thus everybody is required to find out which stone he or she must wear in order to enjoy the utmost good fortune.

As a rule, the stone which any particular person must choose is decided by the month in which that individual was born. But this it not invariably the case. Many people have noticed that luck has come to them when they have been wearing some other stone than that decreed by their birth-month. And, of course, the opposite has often happened. History records a well-known case in point. The Hope diamond, for instance, wrecked the lives of several royal personages, even including some that were born in April; while an opal, possessed by members of the Spanish royal family, brought disaster to many people, one after the other, although certain of them were born in October.

Clearly, then, the proper thing is for all of us to choose our lucky stone according to our own preferences; but failing any definite preference to select it according to the month of our birth.

STONES OF THE MONTHS

Twelve verses of poetry have been written which set down in rhyme the stones for all the months of the year. Here they are:—

JANUARY

By her, who in this month was born,
   No gem save *Garnets* should be worn.
They will ensure her constancy,
   True friendship and fidelity.

FEBRUARY

The February born shall find
   Sincerity and peace of mind,
Freedom from passion and from care,
   If they the *Amethyst* will wear.

MARCH

Who in this world of ours, their eyes
   In March first open, shall be wise,
In days of peril, strong and brave,
   And wear a *Bloodstone* to their grave.

APRIL

Those who from April date their years,
   Should *Diamonds* wear lest bitter tears
For vain repentance flow: this stone,
   Emblem of innocence is known.

MAY

Who first beholds the light of day,
   In spring's sweet, flowery month of May,
And wears an *Emerald* all her life,
   Shall be a loved and loving wife.

JUNE

Who comes in summer to this earth
   And owes to June her time of birth,
With ring of *Agate* on her hand
   Can health, wealth and lengthy life command.

JULY

The glowing *Ruby* shall adorn
   Those who in warm July are born.
Then will they be exempt and free
   From all life's doubts and anxiety.

AUGUST

Wear a *Sardonyx* or for thee
   No conjugal felicity.
The August born without this stone,
   'Tis said, must live unloved alone.

SEPTEMBER

Children born when autumn leaves
   Are rustling in the September breeze,
A *Sapphire* on their brow should bind.
   'Twill cure diseases of the mind.

OCTOBER

October's child is born for woe,
   And life's vicissitudes must know.
But lay an *Opal* on her breast
   And hope will lull those woes to rest.

NOVEMBER

Who comes to this world here below,
   With drear November's fog and snow,
Should prize the *Topaz's* amber hue,
   Emblem of friends and lovers true.

DECEMBER

If cold December gave you birth,
   The month of snow and ice and mirth,
Place on your hand a *Turquoise* blue,
   Success will crown whate'er you do.

AN ABC OF PRECIOUS STONES

AGATE.—A stone, showing irregular bands of browns and yellows, which is often known as onyx, cornelian, etc. It is supposed to have special powers in making and binding friendships. Also, it insures long life, health and prosperity for those born in June.

AMBER.—A brownish material, resembling stone, which is derived from fossilized pine trees. It provides health and happiness when worn round the neck by people born in August.

AMETHYST.—A form of quartz, showing a range of color-shades from purple to lilac. Originally it was worn by the Greeks as a preventive of drunkenness, and, then, as a cure for all excesses of passion. Later, it became the stone associated with St. Valentine. This immediately constituted it the particular charm for lovers. It is the February birthstone.

AQUAMARINE.—A bluish-green form of the beryl or topaz. As the name implies, sea-water, it has long been a mascot for sailors and for those setting out on a long sea journey. It stands for faithfulness: thus it is an appropriate stone for a bridegroom to give to his wife, as a wedding gift.

BERYL.—A pale green stone which is sometimes found with a yellowish tinge. The latter is known as the gold beryl. It is avoided by many people as it stands for doubt, uncertainty and qualities of a wavering nature.

BLOODSTONE.—A stone found with many different colorings and markings. A frequent variety has a greenish surface, sprinkled with patches of vivid red: whilst a totally different variety shows a mottling of red and brown, with streaks of green. The red markings suggested the name of "bloodstone," and the blood became a symbol of bravery, strength and the powers of fighting. Thus, it is a stone to be worn by a man, rather than a lady. In olden days, the women gave bloodstones to their menfolk before going into battle.

CARBUNCLE.—Garnets, when given a round or oval shape, with the surface domed and not cut into facets, are so called.

CHRYSOLITE.—A form of beryl, generally found in colors ranging from olive-green to amber-orange. It is a stone for the September-born and is supposed to banish evil passions and sadness of mind.

CORAL.—A reddish stone, formed by a microscopic animal living in sea water. It is used chiefly for beads. Children wearing such beads are said to be preserved from dangers, whilst married women are ensured a life of happiness. Its powers are chiefly applied to those born in November.

DIAMOND.—A pure form of carbon, water-white in color. The largest known diamond was given to Edward VII, by the Transvaal government in 1907. It weighs one and three-quarter pounds, and is known as the Cullinan diamond. This precious stone is considered to be a symbol of strength and virtue. In olden days, the leaders wore it when going into battle to safeguard their courage. It should be worn on the left side and is the month stone of April.

EMERALD.—This is a delightful variety of green beryl. It has, normally, a brilliant appearance, which is supposed to dwindle should either the giver or the receiver become unfaithful to the other. It stands as a symbol for kindness and true love. It is the month-stone of May.

GARNET.—A ruby-colored stone in the usual form, but there are brown, yellow, green and black varieties. It stands for constancy and fidelity and is the month-stone of January.

JADE.—A very hard stone, usually a rich green, but there are white and other varieties. The Chinese considered that those who wore it would be assured a long and contented life.

JASPER.—An ornamental form of quartz, varying from a reddish-brown to a brownish-black, usually streaked with other colors. It is particularly hard, and this makes it a symbol of firmness and endurance.

LAPIS LAZULI.—This heavenly blue stone is worn as a sign of truth and honesty. The ancients considered that it would charm away certain diseases.

MOONSTONE.—Sometimes called the water opal, this whitish stone reflects a bluish tinge. It is supposed to safeguard those who travel to distant parts, especially if the journey is mostly by sea.

OLIVINE.—A green form of chrysolite, which see.

ONYX.—A form of agate in which the bandings of color are milk-white, alternating with another hue. White and red bands produce the stone known as the cornelian onyx: white and flesh colored bands, chalcedonyx: and white and green bands, sardonyz. The latter is the month-stone of August and stands for conjugal felicity.

OPAL.—A semi-transparent stone, the most usual varieties being whitish in color, but flashing various hues as the angle is changed. The opal has been connected with more legends than, probably, any other stone. To some it is a harbinger of bad luck, but most people agree that it is a stone that brings good fortune to the wearer. It is the month-stone of October. Then it denotes hope, it sharpens the sight and the faith of the possessor. It is supposed to lose its flashing qualities when worn by the unfaithful.

PEARL.—A pearl is a symbol of purity and perfection, and, when given to a lady, is said to inspire her love.

PERIDOT.—A form of olivine or chrysolite. See "Chrysolite."

PORPHYRY.—A stone which usually shows light red or white spots on a background of deep red. There are green varieties, however. This stone, when given to a lady, is a tribute to her beauty.

RUBY.—A stone of deep, clear carmine color, when at its best. It is the month-stone of July, and is supposed to correct evils resulting from mistaken friendships.

SAPPHIRE.—A beautiful blue stone which is reserved for those born in September. It is usually supposed to bring good fortune to those in love, but some people hold that it is a symbol of repentance.

SARDONYX.—See "Onyx."

TOPAZ—A glassy stone, red, blue, yellow or green in color; but amber is the most usual. It is the stone for those born in November, and denotes fidelity and friendship.

TURQUOISE.—A waxy bluish-green stone. It belongs to those born in December and stands for prosperity in love.

ZIRCON.—It is a stone of lustrous grey-black color. It is a symbol of sympathy.

DREAMS—WHAT THEY MEAN

A

ABROAD.—(Dreamer going or gone) An early journey.

ACCIDENT.—(being the victim of one) Business deal impending requires great caution.

ACCIDENT.—(to a friend or relative) A letter from him or her conveying good news.

ANCHOR.—A voyage across the sea: (in water) a disappointment: (if a girl dreams) a sailor will fall in love with her.

ANGER.—To dream of being angry with anyone means that that person is a true friend.

ANIMALS.—As a rule, luck; (domestic animals) speedy return of absent friends, family reconciliation: (wild animals) secret enemies.

APPLES.—Long life: (to a woman) many years and many children.

ARROW.—A letter has been written which will cause regret.

AXE.—A way will present itself soon to attain a much desired end.

B

BALL.—(Game) Money coming soon. (Rolling ball) an unexpected gift of money which will be soon spent.

BALLROOM.—(Dancing with a dear friend) Marriage to him or her.

BANANAS.—A piece of good luck coming.

BAND.—(Musical) A lucky speculation or business deal.

BAREFOOT.—A successful speculation or bargain.

BARREL.—(Full) Money coming quickly.

BATH.—Health and long life: (if dreamer is a young girl) early marriage to present lover.

BATTLE.—(By girl) Will shortly fall in love; (by a soldier) promotion.

BEAR.—(Chasing the dreamer) Victory of an enemy: (bear running from dreamer) victory over an enemy.

BEES.—Steady pursuit of object in view will bring success.

BEGGARS.—To dream of beggars is a fortunate sign to lovers and business people.

BLIND.—To dream of being blind is a very lucky sign; to see a blind person is a warning of danger.

72

BLOOD.—To see blood means great riches, an inheritance.

BOAT.—The arrival of a dear friend.

BOUQUET.—To receive one means much pleasure; to give one, constancy of a lover or friend.

BRACELET.—Good luck and fortune coming.

BROTHER.—Seeing dead brothers or sisters in a dream is a sign of long life.

BULLDOG.—A good omen in love or business.

BURIAL.—To dream of being buried means that wealth is coming—"as much wealth as earth laid over you."

BURNING.—(Houses, etc.) Riches and prosperity.

BUYING.—Happiness and contentment, a legacy.

C

CAGE.—(Birds in) Early fortunate marriage; (empty) friends or lovers will go away.

CAKES.—To dream of any kind of cakes is a good omen.

CANARY.—(Singing) Marriage and a charming house.

CARDS.—(Playing at) Speedy marriage.

CATHEDRAL.—Prosperity and fortune.

CEMETERY.—An omen of prosperity.

CHAIR.—An increase in the family.

CHERRIES.—Good news, pleasure and enjoyment.

CHILDREN.—Lucky omen: increase in wealth.

CHIMNEY.—Good luck, the higher the better.

CHRISTENING.—Good fortune approaching.

COCK CROWING.—Great prosperity.

COINS.—(Copper) Good fortune; (silver) worry; (gold) commercial troubles.

COLD.—Friends will be kind to you.

CORNFIELD.—Health, wealth and pleasant times.

COWS.—Prosperity, the more the better.

D

DAFFODILS.—Pleasure and amusement in abundance.

DAGGER.—A friend will confer a favor.

DEAD.—To dream of oneself as dead is a good and auspicious sign of long life and success.

DEATH OF A FRIEND.—Arrival of good news.

DIGGING.—Good luck with perseverance.

DOCKS.—Good news from abroad.

DOG.—As a rule, a favorable sign; (Dog barking) somebody is trying to do you an ill turn; (Dogs fighting) serious quarrel between two friends of the dreamer.

DONKEY.—Lucky omen, usually a legacy.

DOVES.—Success, especially to lovers. To the married, they denote a pleasure in store.

DROWNING.—(Either the dreamer or another person.) Success, joy, prosperity.

DUCKS.—Increased prosperity and happiness.

E

EAGLE.—Success in a new place.

EARS.—A pleasant letter from a friend.

EATING.—(Dreamer eating) ill luck; (seeing others eat) good luck.

ECHO.—Sickness either of dreamer or relations.

EGGS.—Good luck, money, success; (eggs broken) failure and loss.

ELM TREE.—A good turn offered by a male relative.

ELOPEMENT.—Sign of a speedy marriage.

EMERALD.—A sign of good luck and happiness.

EMPTINESS.—Always a bad sign in a dream.

ENGAGEMENT.—(To dream of being engaged to a handsome person) Great pleasure in store; (to a plain person) worry and trouble.

EYES.—In general a sign of good luck, and the prettier the eyes the better. To dream of someone with a defect of the eyes signifies minor misfortunes.

F

FACES.—(Smiling) Happy times with friends; (pale and gloomy) trouble and poverty; (changing faces) a removal; (washing own face) repentance for sin; (own face in glass) long-cherished secret plan will fail.

FAIRY.—All dreams of fairies are good omens—success and riches.

FALLING.—Indicates some misfortune.

FAN.—Quarrels, a rival in love.

FARMYARD.—Good fortune coming; comfort and happiness.

FEATHERS.—(White) Success and riches; (black) loss and failure.

FENCE.—(Climbing) A sudden rise in life.

FIELDS.—(Green) Prosperity, a happy marriage, handsome children; (clover, barley, wheat, etc.) great prosperity and happiness.

FIGS.—A good dream, joy and pleasure; (if a woman dreams) happy marriage and many children.

FLEET.—(At sea) Realization of cherished hopes.

FLOATING.—To dream of floating on water is a good and lucky sign.

FLOODS.—Success after triumphing over difficulties.

FLOUR.—Death of a relative bringing a legacy.

FLOWERS.—Prosperity.

FLY.—(Swarm of flies) Rivals and jealous persons are spreading scandal.

FLYING—(Without wings) Success in love and business; (if ended by a fall) failure in attaining object; (with wings) bad omen—frustrated ambition.

FOG.—Bad dream—business losses.

FOREIGN.—(Country) Success and prosperity at home.

FOREST.—Trouble and losses through rivals.

FORK.—A warning of imminent danger.

FOUNTAIN.—(Playing) Good luck, happy times and laughter.

FOX.—Trouble through secret enemy; (killing one) good luck.

FRIENDS.—(Absence of) Speedy return; (death of) good news; (illness) bad news; (in good health) their prosperity.

FROGS.—Beware of flatterers and pessimists.

FROST.—Success through aid of friends.

FRUIT.—Usually a good dream, according to kind of fruit; (dreamer eating or throwing away fruit) bad sign.

FUNERAL.—A legacy or a rich marriage.

G

GAS.—Minor discomforts and annoyances.

GATE.—An obstacle to success will suddenly disappear.

GEESE.—Happiness, success; (to hear geese cackling) a profitable business deal will be quickly concluded.

GEMS.—Usually an unfortunate omen.

GHOSTS.—To dream of ghosts is invariably the presage of misfortune.

GIANT.—Good fortune, success in business or love.

GIFTS.—(Receiving) Good fortune coming.

GYPSIES.—A profitless voyage to many strange countries.

GLASS.—To dream of anything made of glass refers to women; (receiving glass of water) birth in the family.

GLOVES.—Usually bad luck; (gloves on hands) honor and safety; (losing gloves) loss in business.

GOAT.—Bad luck, some misfortune, especially unlucky to sailors; (white goat) a profitable venture; (many goats) an inheritance.

GOD.—A good dream—health and happiness.

GOLD.—Omen of loss and bad luck: (dreamer finding gold) a sign that he will be robbed; (dreamer paying out gold) a sign that he will increase the number of his friends.

GOOSEBERRIES.—Time and trouble spent only for the benefit of others.

H

HAIR.—Riches and fine clothes; (hair falling over face) a coming event will cause displeasure; (having hair cut) losses in business; (becoming bald) great danger.

HAMMER.—Triumph over difficulties.

HAMMOCK.—Loss of something that is prized.

HAPPINESS.—A presage of doubt and difficulty.

HARE.—(Alive) Friendship: (dead) good luck: (hare running) a lengthy journey.

HARVEST.—Hopes will not come to fruition.

HAT.—(New) A small success: (blown off or damaged) losses.

HATCHET.—A solution near to existing difficulties.

HAWK.—A happy omen—success in life.

HAY.—Good luck: (dreamer cutting hay) troubles and sorrow.

HAZEL NUT.—(Eating) Troubles and discord.

HEAD.—Good omen—health and money.

HORSESHOE.—(Seeing one) A journey: (finding one) great good luck.

HOSPITAL.—Misery, poverty, wounds.

HOUSE.—Good luck: (dreamer building house) unlucky dream, signifying loss and sickness.

HUNCHBACK.—A troubled life, with many ups and downs.

HUNGER.—To dream of being hungry is a fortunate omen, foretelling that the dreamer, by industry and enterprise, will grow rich.

HUNTING.—(Dreamer returning from a hunt) A fortunate dream: (dreamer going hunting) frustrated hopes and disappointment.

HUSBAND.—For a woman to dream of her husband is not a very favorable dream, usually foretelling discord and deceit: for an unmarried girl to dream that she has a husband is a very bad omen.

HYMNS.—Singing hymns in a dream foretells sickness to the dreamer: (hearing hymns sung) consolation in troubles.

I

IRON.—A profitable bargain: (red-hot) sorrows: (burnt with same) dreamer will receive some personal injury.

ISLAND.—For a woman to dream of an island forebodes desertion by husband or lover.

ITCH.—A sign of good luck.

IVORY.—To dream of anything made of ivory is a sign that the dreamer will suffer from fraud and deception.

IVY.—True friends will present themselves.

J

JEWELS.—To dream of jewelry of any kind is always a bad sign; love troubles or business dangers.

JOCKEY.—(On horseback) A successful speculation or bet.

JOLLITY.—To dream of jollity and fun by night is good for those about to marry: to the poor a sign of good: to the rich a sign of trouble and loss. See "Merry."

JOURNEY.—(Making one) Peace and contentment at home.

JUDGE.—A bad dream: beware of slander and malice.

JUG.—(Drinking from one) Robust health and wholesome pleasures.

JUMP.—To dream of jumping is unpropitious, foretelling obstacles that prevent fulfillment of a desire.

K

KANGAROO.—A secret and powerful enemy or rival.

KENNEL.—An invitation to visit a male friend.

KETTLE.—(Black) An ill omen, death: (copper) lucky dream.

KEY.—Receipt of money: (for young people) a good and handsome partner in life: (holding a key) settlement of business perplexities: (lost key) anger, worry, want.

KILL.—(Dreamer killing a man) Assured happiness: (dreamer being killed) loss to the dream-adversary.

KING.—(Seeing oneself as a King) Warning to beware of flatterers and of self-conceit.

KISS.—Beware of treachery and deceit: (kissing hand of somebody) friendship and good fortune: (kissing a stranger's hand) a journey.

KITCHEN.—Success, advancement in life.

L

LAMP.—(Lit) Trouble, not serious.

LANTERN.—Success: (to see light extinguished or darkened) sadness, sickness, poverty.

LARK.—Good luck: improvement in finances.

LAUGHTER.—Presages difficult circumstances.

LAVENDER.—(To smell or to see it growing) Good luck.

LAWN.—(Looking at) Good health and prosperity: (running on) worry and annoyance.

LAWYER.—Trouble, quarrels, expenses, losses.

LEAD.—An inheritance or legacy from beloved friend.

LEAF.—(To dream of being covered with leaves) Difficulties will prove to be only temporary: (faded leaves) disappointed hopes.

M

MAGPIE.—A bad sign; back-biting and scandal by a false friend.

MAN.—For a young girl to dream about a man is a warning against gossip and gossipers.

MANURE.—Financial gain: good crops.

MAP.—News or visit from a friend abroad.

MARBLE.—An inheritance.

MARRIAGE.—To dream that one marries is a bad, unhappy sign.

MASS.—(Attending Mass) Happiness and health.

MAST.—To dream of tall, towering masts is a sign of prosperity.

MATCHES.—An increase in wealth.

MAYOR.—An elevation to place of dignity and respect.

MEADOW.—A lucky bargain, comfort, and prosperity.

MELANCHOLY.—A presage of mirth and happiness.

MENAGERIE.—Enemies will fail to injure: friends will be true.

MENDING.—(Clothes, etc.) Unhappiness, submission to others.

MERMAID.—Bad luck and misfortune, especially to sailors and those who live by the sea.

MERRY.—(Being) A presage of sadness and gloom.

MESSAGE.—(Receiving one) An advance in life.

MIDWIFE.—An increase in the family.

MILK.—A sign of peaceful circumstances; often means an increase in family: (spilling) loss in business.

MINCE PIES.—(Making) Good luck, a valuable present; (eating) good news.

MINT.—An improvement in health.

MIRROR.—(Married folk dreaming) Children: (young people) sweethearts: (seeing own face) failure of cherished project.

N

NEEDLE.—Love or family quarrels: (unable to thread needle) baseless suspicions causing trouble.

NEGRO.—Unlucky: a warning of trouble.

NEST.—A good omen: fortunate love: happy family life.

NETTLES.—(Stung by them) Sign that the dreamer will make a bold effort to reach a desired end or gain a desired object; for young people to dream thus is a sign that they are in love and wishful to enter the unknown and, possibly, unhappy state of matrimony.

NEWSPAPERS.—(Reading them) A presage of news from a foreign country.

NIGHT.—To dream of night presages sadness and gloom.

NIGHTINGALE.—(Hearing nightingales sing) Joyfulness, success in business, good crops, a happy marriage to a good and faithful mate: (for a married woman to dream) she will have children who will become great singers.

NIGHTMARE.—To dream of having a nightmare is a sign that the dreamer will be immediately married, and (if a man) his wife will turn out a shrew.

NINE.—To see objects or persons to the number of nine intensifies or multiplies the effect, nine being the superlative of superlatives.

NOISE.—Hearing loud, discordant noises, particularly if their source is not apparent, is a bad omen.

P

PEARLS.—Weeping and tears, hard times, worry, and treason.

PEARS.—(Gathering them) Pleasant companionship and enjoyment: (eating them) sickness and possibly death.

PEAS.—(Seeing them growing) Fortunate enterprises: (cooked) good and speedy success and enjoyment of well-gained riches.

PEBBLES.—Sorrows and troubles: (young woman dreams) she will be made unhappy by attractive rivals.

PEDDLER.—Beware of false friends.

PEN.—Avoid a friend whose example and advice are bad.

PERFUME.—An augury of success and happiness.

PERSPIRATION.—To dream of being bathed in perspiration foretells the inception of some arduous task which will be successfully achieved.

PETTICOAT.—A bad dream portending troubles caused by frivolity, to a man: and to a woman vexations through vanity and pride.

PIANO—(Playing or seeing another play) The death of relations, funeral obsequies.

PIG.—Good luck, reasonable success in affairs.

PICTURE.—To dream of painting pictures denotes that you will engage in some unremunerative, albeit not unpleasant, enterprise.

PIGEON.—Domestic peace and comfort, success in exterior affairs. Wild pigeons signify dissolute women: tame pigeons, honest women and wives.

PINE-TREE.—Continual happiness and vigorous old age.

PINS.—Differences and quarrels in families.

PIT.—(Falling in) Disappointment in love, misfortunes, danger: (being in, but climbing out) a difficulty overcome.

PLOUGH.—A good omen in love, courtship and marriage, though the good may be rather slow in coming.

R

RABBIT.—(White) Success: (black) worry.

RACE.—To see oneself winning a race is a good omen, except to sick persons.

RACES.—Bad luck: losses by trickery and swindling of low persons.

RAGS.—(Being dressed in) Success and prosperity after much striving.

RAILWAY.—A journey: (accident) a break in friendship.

RAIN.—A lucky omen: an inheritance, prosperity, good crops: (heavy storm) troubles and difficulties.

RAINBOW.—Change of residence or manner of life: (if seen on the right hand) a change for the better: (if on the left) an "Irishman's rise."

RAT.—Treachery from inferiors: (white rat) good fortune.

RAVEN.—Bad luck to the business man, disappointment to the lover, separation to the married.

RAZOR.—An unhappy portent: love quarrels.

S

SNAKE, SERPENT.—Bad luck, sickness, short life.

SNOW.—Success, money, plentiful harvest: (eating snow) the dreamer will soon undertake a difficult journey: (lost in snow) hostilities of enemies.

SOAP.—A way out of pressing difficulties will present itself.

SOWING.—An indication of doubtful enterprises.

SPADE.—To dream of using a spade is a sign that the dreamer will commit indiscretions which he will endeavor to hide.

SPARROW.—Troubles: (many) an early journey: (sparrow struggling to escape) a foreboding of mischief.

SPECTACLES.—Be on guard against persons trying to deceive.

SPECTRE.—An omen of misfortune and disaster.

SPIDER.—Good luck, successful schemes: (killing one) a very bad omen.

SPINNING.—Worry and trouble in which strangers are mixed.

STABLE.—Prepare for the visit of a true friend.

STAIN.—(To dream of rubbing out stains which reappear) Retribution and punishment for sin.

T

TABLE.—(Sitting at) A sign of comfort and prosperity, a happy marriage.

TEA.—Trouble that will cause sleeplessness and bad health.

TEAR.—To dream of tearing paper while reading is a sign that business perplexities will be smoothed away.

TEARS.—A presage of great joy and merriment.

TEETH.—In a dream teeth denote relatives, the two front teeth representing children, brothers or sisters, and others are distant relations. Losing a tooth is a sign of death of a relative: the loss of all in any way means that the dreamer will outlive all his family.

THIEVES.—A warning against gossipers and tattlers.

THIMBLE.—The loss of employment.

THREAD.—Beware of intrigues: (breaking) poverty: (entangling the thread of a spool or skein) difficulties, perplexities, business troubles.

W

WALK.—(Alone and slowly) A sign of poverty and sadness: (fast) success in a desired object: (through fire) danger: (on water or on the sea) bad luck: (with somebody else) enjoyment of comfort and companionship: (girl to walk with her lover) a comfortable and happy marriage.

WALL.—Many obstacles in realizing a future plan: (climbing over or destroying) obstacles successfully surmounted: (jumping over) joy and happiness.

WASH.—(Body) Release from anxieties: (clothes) a presage of hard and unrequited toil for others.

WASPS.—Vexation and troubles caused by envious persons.

WATCH.—Gains, money, prosperity.

WATER.—(Clear) Comfort and happiness: (dirty) sorrow and trouble: (stagnant) severe illness, probably ending with death: (very cold) beware of enemies: (hot) illness: (seeing in improbable places or circumstances) trouble and danger: (dried up or disturbed) an improvement in affairs: (gushing up from below) a sign of unsuspected enemies: (carrying it in a sieve or other unlikely receptacle without spilling) much domestic trouble, disappointment, great losses: (another person doing so) good luck to the dreamer or to that person, or good luck to the dreamer in connection with that person: (drinking clear water) a lucky sign, comfort and satisfaction.

TEACUP FORTUNETELLING

(In the following pages, you may learn something of the meanings attached to the tea leaves which remain among the dregs in the bottom of your teacup.)

HOW TO TEST YOUR FORTUNES

Leave a slight amount of tea in the cup, not so much as a spoonful. Place the saucer on the cup, swill the cup round, males do this so that the liquid moves round in a clockwise direction, females in an anti-clockwise direction. The tea is then run out of the cup, the saucer lifted off and the shapes or formations are ready to be examined.

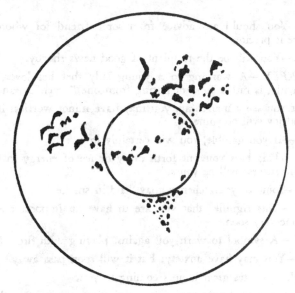

No. 17.—Birds seen in tea leaves generally denote an end of your troubles.

WHAT THE FORMATIONS MEAN

ANCHOR.—Denotes a voyage full of hope. It is considered a splendid omen for a sailor's bride.

ARCH.—You are to undertake a journey in the near future. It is sometimes a happy omen for a woman, signifying that she will marry a tall, handsome man and be blessed with healthy children.

AXE.—Denotes that your difficulties have now been overcome by your own splendid endeavors. You have severed the old bad habits and made a clean cut at your past blunders.

BALLOON.—Although it denotes a certain rise in the consultant's fortunes, it carries the warning to beware of a sudden fall.

BANANA.—Signifies to the sick, quick restoration to health.

BASKET.—Implies that a person, by changing his or her mind within the last twenty-four hours, has reason for congratulation.

BELLS.—If they are connected to a rope, you can look forward to splendid news.

BIRDS.—Generally, they denote an end of your troubles.

BOAT.—If you cannot discover an occupant of the boat, the symbol means a voyage.

BOOK.—You should ask advice from some friend for whom you care. Good advice is precious.

BUGLE.—You will be the recipient of good news shortly.

BUTTERFLY.—A warning to a young lady that her lover, whom she trusts implicitly, is rather fond of flitting from one "peach" to another.

CAP.—If you see a man's cap, you may have minor worries: if a widow's cap, married joy will be yours.

CARDS.—If you gamble, you will certainly lose.

CHAIN.—This bids you put forth every ounce of energy in one big endeavor: then, success will be yours.

CIGAR.—Some of your schemes may "end in smoke."

CLOCK.—This signifies that you are to have an important appointment with someone very soon.

COMET.—A symbol to warn you against playing with fire. Beware.

CROSS.—You may have anxiety: but it will soon pass away.

CROWN.—Denotes great honors coming to you.

DART.—You will shortly have a proposal of marriage. Cupid is about.

DICE.—You will lose money if you gamble.

DOVES.—Your trials will end when you see this welcome "messenger of peace."

ENVELOPE.—Good tidings are heralded.

EYE.—Look to some other power than your own.

FINGERPRINT.—A reminder to you to ask and you will find out a secret.

FISH.—This signifies good news from abroad. If the fish is surrounded by dots you will emigrate.

FLAG.—A splendid omen—the best of news is coming from abroad, and you are about to experience good fortune at home.

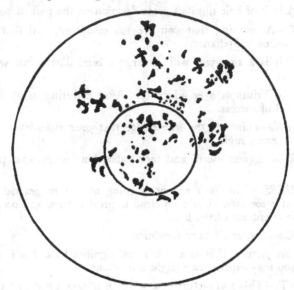

No. 18.—Cross. You may have anxiety, but it will soon pass away.

FOOT.—This leaf-picture denotes good news which, however, is still far off.

FORK.—Your life would be all the happier were you not so easily flattered.

GALLOWS.—Contrary to expectation, to see this picture denotes nothing of evil significance, but is merely a warning to you to be cautious—in fact, a kindly symbol.

GARDEN.—Prosperous, joyful days.

GATE.—A reminder that patience is a virtue, and that the gate to fortune will open for you in due course.

GIANT.—This denotes you are attempting something which is far too big for you. Better be a successful dwarf than a gigantic failure.

GYPSY.—An invitation to you to wish for something you dearly desire, and your wish will be granted.

GLOBE.—Denotes you are to take a roundabout journey leading finally to your home.

GLOVE.—A sign of good luck.

GOOSE.—You will be the recipient of foolish remarks from stupid persons, but these need cause you no concern.

GRAPES.—From time immemorial the symbol of perfect love between couples.

HAIR.—A lock of hair signifies great devotion on the part of your lover.

HALTER.—A warning that you are too easily led, and that you must cultivate the art of self-reliance.

HAM.—This is a sign you will undergo a brief illness, but will make a quick recovery.

HAMMER.—Triumph over adversity. After enduring many knocks you will hit the nail of success.

HAMMOCK.—Points to the knowledge that your sailor-lover is true and dreams of you every night.

HAMPER.—Suggests useful and serviceable, but inexpensive, presents are coming.

HANDCUFFS.—This is a cogent warning to you to get rid of an evil habit before it is too late. Little sins lead to great crimes, and no one desires to receive the attentions of the law.

HARP.—Count yourself very fortunate.

HAT.—This picture, if it is a lady's hat, signifies luck, but if a man's, it means that you may experience a slight misfortune.

HATCHET.—This leaf-picture is a warning to take great care or you may experience danger.

INITIAL.—In this important leaf-picture the initials should be carefully studied. If the initial is formed near the rim, the significance is one of good fortune. Initials most commonly found are those without curves. Such straight initials are—A, I, L, N, T, V, W.

INTERROGATION MARK.—Signifies doubt. Be careful.

KEY.—An important picture suggesting that you look deeper and more carefully in the cup for an initial, which, when you have found it, will unlock something that has been up till now a mystery. A closed book will be opened for you and past enigmas unravelled.

LABEL.—This ticket-like picture, which must not be mistaken for an envelope, is the sign that you possess a dear friend who will one day be "tied" to you for life.

LACE.—Denotes you will err on a very minor and fragile matter and make a false move on very flimsy grounds.

LADDER.—If on the side of the cup a rise in your fortunes is indicated.

LADY.—Points to the fact that you will shortly make a friend of one who will prove of great service.

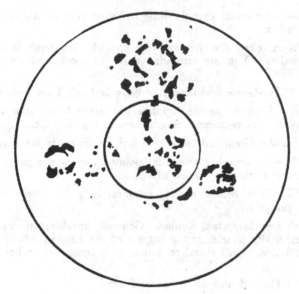

No. 19.—A Mark of Interrogation signifies doubt: be careful.

LINES.—These indicate journeys.

LOCK.—This denotes that you can safely confide in your nearest friend. He or she will lock your secrets in his or her bosom.

LOCKET.—A picture denoting steadfast loyalty on the part of a friend whom you have not seen for long months.

LOOKING GLASS.—You are warned by this picture that the world sees you for what you really are. Your character is mirrored for your friends to gaze upon.

MAN.—Denotes a visitor who will bring a gift if his arm is outstretched. If the symbol is clear he is a dark man; if vague he is very fair.

MAP.—A symbol bidding you travel, for you will be sure of success wherever you go.

MAZE.—A regular "maze of difficulty" confronts you, but with care you will find a way out of the labyrinth.

MILESTONES.—You are about to win success after traveling a long and difficult road.

MOON.—If shown as a crescent prosperity and fortune are indicated.

MOTORCAR.—Denotes that you will achieve a rapid success.

MOUNTAINS.—This majestic picture signifies an arduous, lengthy, and uphill fight against bad fortune. Set your heart to it, and toil on to the goal.

MOUSE.—A reminder that the little irritation you are nursing is really a very trivial affair.

NAVVY.—A token that you are very bookish, and fond of digging into abstruse treatises. You are reminded that "all work and no play makes Jack a dull boy."

NECKLACE.—Grace and beauty of body and mind are here indicated.

NEEDLE.—A single needle signifies you are able to withstand all the sharp pricks of circumstances. Several needles together mean quarrels.

PENDULUM.—Great indecision and lack of character are here indicated.

PENNON.—To decipher this small-pointed flag is a sign that someone on board a ship is thinking much of you.

PENNIES.—They denote great carefulness in small details, which leads to ultimate prosperity.

RING.—A very important symbol. Generally speaking, it always denotes marriage, especially if seen at the bottom of the cup, in which case search for an initial which will reveal to a man or woman his or her future life-partner.

RIVERS.—These denote much peace of mind.

ROADS.—If the roads appear in the clear they predict a speedy change of circumstances, usually for the better.

ROBIN.—This bird always denotes hope. If you see it you can cheer up, as the trouble you now experience is about to pass away.

ROCK.—A massive rock denotes great burdens. If there are a number of small rocks easy fortune and much happiness are indicated.

ROCKET.—Another warning against high ambition.

ROD.—If it is long and slender you will be very fortunate.

ROOF.—If what appears to be the roof only of a house is seen the signification is domestic bliss.

ROOK.—Great happiness is indicated.

SAILOR.—Foretells that very shortly you will receive a letter from over the sea.

SCALES.—This picture is the token that the friend you have weighed in the balance and found wanting is really true and just.

SCEPTRE.—A sign of honor from royalty.

SERPENT.—If on the side of the cup and appearing to be rising to near the brim you may take comfort in the fact that you will shortly receive some information which will be of use.

SHEAVES.—A good omen of a bounteous harvest of prosperity.

SHIELD.—A reminder that you have just escaped from a great calamity.

SHIP.—A large ship with funnels and masts is a token of a long journey, usually on business.

THIMBLE.—This homely picture denotes that industry and devotion to duty bring their own reward.

THIN PERSON.—The figure of a very slender person is usually the sign of very prosperous days ahead.

THISTLE.—This striking leaf-picture is a sign that you will only achieve success by plain living and high thinking.

THORN.—This is always an excellent omen. Good luck and many friends are indicated.

TONGS.—Suggests you are of a fiery nature, and will quarrel with your best friend.

TONGUE.—Someone you are fond of who is far away is speaking about you.

TOOL.—Any instrument of manual operation denotes that hard knocks may be coming.

TRIANGLE.—This is a token of all-round prosperity in love.

TRIDENT.—This is a token of success and honors in the Navy.

WAGON.—A reminder that you are soon to undertake a long journey.

WAITER.—This picture denotes that riches and married happiness will come to you.

WALKING STICK.—A warning not to lean too much on your own efforts.

WATERFALL.—Indicates the removal of many obstructions in your path to happiness.

WEATHERCOCK.—This picture points to a friend who is unreliable.

WEB.—Signifies you will one day be caught in the toils as the result of ignoring friendly warnings.

WELL.—This denotes you are not dipping deep enough into knowledge.

WHEN WILL YOU MARRY?

It has long been held that an unmarried person can tell how many years it will be before he or she is married, in the following manner.

Balance a small spoon on the edge of a teacup. The spoon should be perfectly dry. Then, with the assistance of a second spoon, tilt drops of tea into the balancing spoon and count them, one by one. The number of drops it takes to upset the spoon reveals the number of years that will elapse before the wedding takes place.

LUCKY AND UNLUCKY DAYS

Most of us have discovered that certain days of the week, or even the year, are more favorable to us than others. But there are some people who have not made this discovery. To them, the indications given in this chapter will be of considerable interest.

Friday—an Unlucky Day.—Fortunately, six of the seven days of the week are charitably disposed towards the majority of us. Here and there, a person may be found who affirms that Monday, Thursday or some other day never did him or her a kindness; but such a remark is not general. Friday, however, can be put on the black list, as it is a notoriously unlucky day. Most men and women cherish a superstitious fear of it, and this opinion has existed since the first Good Friday. Many will never embark upon any enterprise of importance; there are fewer marriages on this day than any other, and sailors are averse to sailing on Friday. Many are the tales they tell of vessels which put to sea on a Friday, and were never heard of again. If all the bank or financial crashes of the last century were counted up, it would be found that Friday supplied the greatest number. A lengthy list could be added to prove that Friday is a day of bad luck.

One good thing can be said for it, however—it favors its own: for people born on a Friday are not affected by its evil disposition.

Unlucky Dates.—In an old calendar, astrologers indicated the following dates as unlucky. If any of them fell on a Friday, they were doubly unlucky:

January 1, 2, 4, 5, 10, 17, 29—very unlucky.
February 26, 27, 28—unlucky; 8, 10, 17—very unlucky.
March 16, 17, 20—very unlucky.
April 7, 8, 10, 20—unlucky; 16 and 21—very unlucky.
June 10 and 22—unlucky; 4 and 8—very unlucky.
July 15 and 21—very unlucky.
August 1, 29 and 30—unlucky; 19 and 20—very unlucky.
September 2, 4, 21, 23—unlucky; 6 and 7—very unlucky.
October 4, 16, 24—unlucky; 6, very unlucky.
November 5, 6, 29, 30—unlucky; 15 and 20—very unlucky.
December 15, 22—unlucky; 6, 7, and 9—very unlucky.

These were regarded as perilous days to fall ill upon, to have an accident, to be married, to start on a journey, or commence any work.

What is most striking about this list is that the "thirteenth" does not appear on it at all, although most people will tell you that the thirteenth is the date they avoid more than all others.

Lucky and Unlucky Dates depending on Birth-dates.—Much the most accurate way of determining which dates are lucky and unlucky is by using the portents displayed by the Signs of the Zodiac. To do this, it is necessary to know when the individual affected was born. The following is a list worked out on these lines:

91

Born—Dec. 22nd to Jan. 20th.

Lucky Dates:		Unlucky Dates:	
Jan.	2, 7, 8, 18, 26 and 31	Jan.	11, 14, 15 and 28
Feb.	3, 7, 9, 12, 13 and 27	Feb.	11, 18, 24 and 25
Mar.	1, 5, 7, 10, 24 and 28	Mar.	8, 16, 17 and 23
April	2, 3, 7, 16, 25 and 26	April	12, 13, 19 and 20
May	5, 6, 14, 15, 27 and 31	May	10, 16, 29 and 30
June	1, 14, 15, 18, 24 and 29	June	5, 13, 22 and 26
July	9, 12, 13, 17, 20 and 27	July	2, 11, 16 and 24
Aug.	3, 8, 9, 16, 21 and 31	Aug.	6, 18, 19 and 29
Sept.	5, 9, 14, 18, 19 and 27	Sept.	1, 3, 17 and 23
Oct.	10, 11, 16, 17, 25 and 30	Oct.	8, 12, 21 and 27
Nov.	6, 7, 8, 12, 13 and 26	Nov.	10, 17, 18 and 25
Dec.	3, 8, 9, 19, 24 and 31	Dec.	2, 6, 11 and 30

Born—Jan. 21st to Feb. 19th

Lucky Dates:		Unlucky Dates:	
Jan.	1, 5, 9, 10, 15 and 20	Jan.	2, 19, 24 and 31
Feb.	2, 5, 6, 11, 16 and 29	Feb.	13, 20, 26 and 27
Mar.	3, 6, 7, 10, 17 and 30	Mar.	11, 19, 24 and 25
April	4, 5, 10, 20, 23 and 29	April	7, 14, 15 and 24
May	7, 8, 16, 17, 25 and 31	May	4, 12, 18 and 19
June	5, 12, 17, 18, 25 and 26	June	1, 2, 28 and 29
July	10, 11, 19, 22, 23 and 28	July	5, 12, 13 and 26
Aug.	10, 14, 19, 20, 24 and 25	Aug.	2, 22, 23 and 27
Sept.	10, 11, 12, 22, 29 and 30	Sept.	4, 5, 19 and 25
Oct.	1, 3, 9, 13, 27 and 28	Oct.	2, 8, 11 and 26
Nov.	4, 5, 10, 15, 23 and 28	Nov.	11, 18, 26 and 27
Dec.	7, 8, 13, 21, 25 and 27	Dec.	9, 16, 17 and 24

Born—Feb. 20th to March 20th

	Lucky Dates:		Unlucky Dates:
Jan.	5, 7, 9, 21, 22 and 27	Jan.	8, 16, 23 and 28
Feb.	4, 7, 9, 20, 21 and 26	Feb.	5, 10, 22 and 25
Mar.	5, 6, 12, 13, 17 and 29	Mar.	11, 15, 18 and 26
April	6, 8, 11, 15, 22 and 30	April	9, 12, 20 and 23
May	8, 14, 15, 19, 24 and 29	May	4, 17, 20 and 28
June	10, 11, 19, 21, 23 and 27	June	6, 18, 24 and 28
July	11, 15, 20, 22, 24 and 31	July	8, 21, 25 and 26
Aug.	13, 16, 17, 20, 28 and 30	Aug.	4, 5, 19 and 25
Sept.	15, 17, 19, 24, 27 and 28	Sept.	3, 8, 18 and 26
Oct.	17, 19, 20, 21, 29 and 30	Oct.	4, 6, 8 and 28
Nov.	8, 9, 10, 14, 19 and 21	Nov.	1, 12, 18 and 24
Dec.	3, 7, 9, 13, 22 and 28	Dec.	11, 16, 20 and 29

Born—March 21st to April 19th

	Lucky Dates:		Unlucky Dates:
Jan.	1, 5, 9, 23, 27 and 28	Jan.	6, 16, 26 and 29
Feb.	2, 5, 10, 19, 25 and 29	Feb.	8, 15, 16 and 23
Mar.	4, 9, 10, 19, 20 and 31	Mar.	3, 6, 15 and 21
April	1, 5, 14, 15, 19 and 28	April	2, 3, 17 and 30
May	3, 12, 13, 18, 21 and 31	May	8, 14, 27 and 28
June	3, 7, 17, 18, 25 and 27	June	4, 5, 23 and 26
July	1, 6, 14, 23, 28 and 29	July	2, 4, 30 and 31
Aug.	2, 10, 11, 24, 25 and 26	Aug.	6, 12, 22 and 23
Sept.	7, 10, 11, 12, 21 and 25	Sept.	2, 23, 24 and 26
Oct.	3, 9, 13, 17, 19 and 31	Oct.	6, 14, 26 and 27
Nov.	1, 5, 8, 14, 20 and 30	Nov.	6, 18, 22 and 29
Dec.	1, 13, 25, 26, 27 and 31	Dec.	6, 12, 22 and 28

Born—April 20th to May 20th

	Lucky Dates:		Unlucky Dates:
Jan.	5, 7, 11, 15, 17 and 25	Jan.	2, 10, 24 and 30
Feb.	3, 5, 6, 7, 24 and 28	Feb.	19, 20, 22 and 23
Mar.	1, 10, 17, 19, 20 and 29	Mar.	3, 24, 25 and 28
April	3, 7, 12, 24, 25 and 29	April	14, 16, 19 and 27
May	1, 5, 6, 9, 23 and 27	May	11, 13, 24 and 26
June	1, 5, 9, 14, 15 and 27	June	3, 6, 18 and 19
July	2, 7, 8, 17, 21 and 31	July	5, 6, 18 and 20
Aug.	12, 13, 14, 22, 26 and 31	Aug.	1, 9, 28 and 29
Sept.	1, 12, 22, 26, 27 and 30	Sept.	5, 11, 25 and 29
Oct.	5, 6, 7, 20, 21 and 26	Oct.	10, 11, 24 and 25
Nov.	3, 7, 8, 13, 22 and 29	Nov.	5, 9, 20 and 27
Dec.	3, 5, 13, 20, 25 and 31	Dec.	1, 12, 22 and 28

Born—May 21st to June 21st

	Lucky Dates:		Unlucky Dates:
Jan.	1, 9, 19, 20, 27 and 28	Jan.	4, 5, 11 and 26
Feb.	5, 6, 11, 21, 23 and 25	Feb.	1, 2, 28 and 29
Mar.	6, 9, 15, 20, 30 and 31	Mar.	7, 19, 28 and 29
April	1, 5, 7, 16, 17 and 24	April	15, 19, 20 and 22
May	3, 6, 7, 17, 24 and 25	May	14, 21, 23 and 26
June	3, 7, 9, 13, 25 and 26	June	11, 16, 17 and 27
July	2, 9, 10, 19, 23 and 29	July	7, 8, 15 and 20
Aug.	7, 14, 21, 24, 25 and 27	Aug.	4, 11, 17 and 22
Sept.	3, 11, 12, 17, 21 and 26	Sept.	1, 6, 14 and 22
Oct.	1, 9, 17, 19, 23 and 28	Oct.	5, 8, 11 and 27
Nov.	5, 9, 15, 23, 24 and 30	Nov.	3, 7, 22 and 28
Dec.	1, 7, 11, 12, 21 and 25	Dec.	5, 6, 19 and 27

Born—June 22nd to July 22nd

	Lucky Dates:		Unlucky Dates:
Jan.	3, 9, 11, 13, 16 and 29	Jan.	6, 8, 27 and 28
Feb.	7, 8, 13, 14, 22 and 27	Feb.	3, 11, 24 and 25
Mar.	5, 7, 12, 20, 21 and 25	Mar.	1, 4, 22 and 26
April	2, 7, 8, 12, 13 and 29	April	5, 19, 20 and 25
May	1, 5, 10, 11, 18 and 19	May	3, 17, 23 and 30
June	2, 7, 10, 15, 24 and 28	June	13, 19, 20 and 22
July	3, 4, 7, 20, 22 and 25	July	10, 13, 23 and 28
Aug.	5, 8, 9, 21, 22 and 30	Aug.	7, 12, 19 and 20
Sept.	5, 12, 13, 19, 27 and 28	Sept.	3, 10, 16 and 17
Oct.	1, 3, 11, 15, 16 and 30	Oct.	7, 14, 27 and 28
Nov.	6, 7, 16, 17, 27 and 30	Nov.	8, 9, 18 and 19
Dec.	4, 9, 13, 24, 30 and 31	Dec.	6, 7, 18 and 21

Born—July 23rd to August 21st

	Lucky Dates:		Unlucky Dates:
Jan.	1, 4, 13, 15, 18 and 27	Jan.	3, 8, 12 and 30
Feb.	1, 15, 20, 24, 25 and 29	Feb.	8, 12, 21 and 28
Mar.	9, 18, 19, 20, 21 and 28	Mar.	12, 22, 24 and 25
April	1, 5, 10, 11, 18 and 23	April	7, 8, 16 and 22
May	2, 3, 6, 12, 13 and 31	May	5, 18, 19 and 24
June	3, 4, 13, 17, 26 and 30	June	2, 14, 21 and 22
July	2, 6, 9, 14, 23 and 29	July	12, 13, 24 and 25
Aug.	3, 7, 10, 23, 25 and 30	Aug.	9, 14, 21 and 22
Sept.	3, 15, 16, 22, 26 and 29	Sept.	5, 17, 18 and 19
Oct.	1, 13, 17, 27, 28 and 31	Oct.	9, 14, 15 and 29
Nov.	9, 10, 15, 20, 23 and 27	Nov.	5, 12, 13 and 17
Dec.	7, 11, 16, 18, 22 and 26	Dec.	3, 9, 23 and 28

Born—August 22nd to September 22nd

	Lucky Dates:		Unlucky Dates:
Jan.	1, 3, 9, 15, 20 and 31	Jan.	4, 11, 18 and 19
Feb.	3, 12, 13, 18, 23 and 27	Feb.	8, 15, 16 and 29
Mar.	1, 11, 20, 21, 28 and 29	Mar.	6, 7, 26 and 27
April	7, 8, 15, 17, 24 and 25	April	2, 3, 9 and 29
May	4, 7, 10, 18, 22 and 31	May	8, 21, 27 and 28
June	1, 6, 7, 11, 15 and 29	June	3, 9, 16 and 24
July	4, 9, 10, 17, 25 and 30	July	2, 14, 20 and 22
Aug.	3, 5, 12, 22, 28 and 29	Aug.	10, 17, 18 and 23
Sept.	4, 9, 10, 22, 23 and 28	Sept.	7, 8, 17 and 21
Oct.	1, 2, 11, 12, 25 and 30	Oct.	4, 8, 14 and 20
Nov.	17, 18, 22, 23, 25 and 30	Nov.	5, 7, 12 and 21
Dec.	9, 10, 18, 23, 26 and 28	Dec.	4, 5, 6 and 14

Born—September 23rd to October 23rd

	Lucky Dates:		Unlucky Dates:
Jan.	1, 5, 9, 19, 20 and 27	Jan.	6, 7, 21 and 23
Feb.	2, 6, 15, 20, 24 and 29	Feb.	11, 17, 19 and 22
Mar.	4, 14, 18, 23, 27 and 31	Mar.	2, 9, 10 and 28
April	1, 15, 19, 23, 24 and 28	April	4, 5, 14 and 26
May	7, 8, 12, 17, 21 and 24	May	3, 9, 23 and 29
June	8, 12, 13, 16, 22 and 30	June	7, 19, 20 and 27
July	4, 14, 19, 20, 23 and 28	July	10, 17, 27 and 29
Aug.	1, 7, 10, 11, 15 and 30	Aug.	12, 13, 22 and 27
Sept.	3, 6, 11, 20, 22 and 29	Sept.	8, 16, 17 and 24
Oct.	4, 5, 17, 22, 24 and 27	Oct.	8, 12, 20 and 21
Nov.	1, 4, 6, 14, 19 and 26	Nov.	9, 17, 28 and 29
Dec.	3, 12, 13, 21, 25 and 29	Dec.	4, 7, 15 and 19

Born—October 24th to November 22nd

	Lucky Dates:		Unlucky Dates:
Jan.	2, 3, 7, 8, 22 and 30	Jan.	10, 16, 18 and 24
Feb.	3, 9, 17, 18, 24 and 27	Feb.	1, 12, 14 and 20
Mar.	1, 6, 15, 20, 25 and 29	Mar.	3, 11, 19 and 30
April	2, 3, 12, 17, 21 and 29	April	7, 8, 26 and 28
May	5, 10, 11, 15, 19 and 27	May	4, 6, 24 and 26
June	6, 11, 15, 19, 23 and 25	June	2, 8, 26 and 28
July	4, 7, 9, 17, 21 and 30	July	3, 8, 19 and 31
Aug.	5, 9, 13, 17, 18 and 27	Aug.	2, 12, 22 and 28
Sept.	9, 10, 12, 23, 27 and 28	Sept.	11, 14, 18 and 29
Oct.	2, 3, 11, 20, 25 and 29	Oct.	8, 9, 22 and 24
Nov.	2, 6, 16, 17, 23 and 30	Nov.	5, 12, 18 and 29
Dec.	2, 5, 18, 19, 24 and 27	Dec.	3, 6, 16 and 18

Born—November 23rd to December 21st

	Lucky Dates:		Unlucky Dates:
Jan.	1, 9, 14, 15, 23 and 24	Jan.	6, 12, 18 and 22
Feb.	3, 5, 7, 19, 21 and 28	Feb.	8, 15, 16 and 23
Mar.	5, 8, 10, 19, 23 and 31	Mar.	6, 7, 15 and 21
April	4, 14, 15, 19, 20 and 28	April	3, 18, 22 and 26
May	1, 12, 16, 20, 26 and 31	May	7, 14, 15 and 27
June	7, 8, 13, 17, 21 and 25	June	3, 11, 23 and 24
July	6, 11, 15, 21, 22 and 25	July	7, 20, 23 and 29
Aug.	3, 6, 7, 14, 15 and 29	Aug.	4, 12, 18 and 28
Sept.	1, 10, 12, 15, 26 and 29	Sept.	13, 17, 20 and 22
Oct.	4, 5, 22, 23, 27 and 31	Oct.	11, 12, 18 and 26
Nov.	9, 19, 20, 23, 24 and 28	Nov.	6, 14, 15 and 22
Dec.	3, 7, 8, 17, 22 and 25	Dec.	6, 11, 18 and 28

It should be noted in connection with the above figures that no birth-date is unlucky. Thus, should any particular reader find that his birthday is given as unlucky, he may transfer it immediately to the list of lucky dates. As an example, take the last line of unlucky figures, given above. They are Dec. 6, 11, 18 and 28, and they operate for people born between Nov. 23rd and Dec. 21st. Should a person born on Dec. 6th be consulting this list, the only unlucky dates in December for him or her are Dec. 11, 18 and 28.

THE LUCK OF FLOWERS

It has been a favorite pastime with maidens in all ages to try to foretell their future by the aid of flowers and plants.

One of the most popular fancies is provided by the four-leaved clover, the story of which is told in various legends. One runs to the effect that three beautiful sisters, Faith, Hope and Charity, came from over the seas, and wherever they walked three-leaved clovers, crimson, white and yellow, bloomed profusely. In their footsteps came another more beautiful being, whose name was Love, and in his honor the clover added a fourth petal to the trefoil.

In time, it became the talisman of love-sick maidens, who wore it in their shoe to ensure a speedy meeting with their sweetheart, wore it over their heart to frighten away evil spirits and to prevent being jilted. In the case of a quarrel, it served to effect a reconciliation.

Apart from its sentimental associations, a four-leaved clover has long been regarded as an emblem of good luck, and has been worn by those who believe in such things when they wished to increase their chances of good fortune.

SPRING FLOWERS.—Naturally, many beliefs flourish around the flowers of the garden and the hedgerow.

If you chance to find the first flower of the season on a Monday, it means good luck.

If on a Tuesday, big undertakings are likely to be successful.

If on a Wednesday, it denotes your approaching wedding.

If on a Thursday, hard work with little profit will fall to your lot.

If on a Friday, unexpected wealth reaches you.

If on a Saturday, you may look out for misfortune.

If on a Sunday, phenomenal good luck will come to you.

THE FIRST WILD FLOWER.—From the first wild flowers which you gather in spring, it is possible to discover the initials of your future husband or wife. If, for instance, they should chance to be daisies, violets and butter-cups, then expect to find some suitable person with the initials D. V. B., but they may not be necessarily in this order.

If someone presents you with a yellow flower, then you may expect a gift of money directly.

If you can turn a bluebell inside out without breaking it, then your lover will be true as long as both of you live.

THE PANSY.—If you wish to know your future destiny, pluck a pansy, which takes its name from *pensee,* a thought. Count the streaks or lines upon the petals.

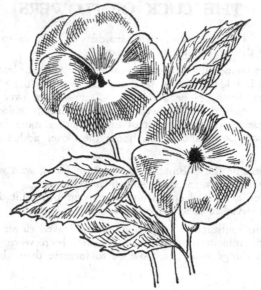

No. 21.

Four streaks tell that your dearest wish will be fulfilled.

Five streaks stand for hope with fear.

Six streaks suggest a surprise.

Seven streaks tell of constancy in your lover.

Eight streaks, fickleness.

Nine streaks, a change and then riches.

Markings leaning towards the left denote trouble.

Markings leaning to the right denote prosperity.

Should the central streak be the longest, then Sunday should be chosen as your wedding day.

THE DAISY.—One of the oldest of flower charms is to pluck at the petals of a daisy or marguerite. At first pluck, these words are said, "He loves me"; at the second, "He loves me not." These sentences are repeated alternately until the flower is deprived of all its petals. Whichever sentence was uttered last describes "his" affections.

THE IVY.—Ivy, ivy, I thee pluck,
 And in my bosom, I thee put.
 The first young man who speaks to me
 My own true lover he shall be.

No. 22.

THE HAWTHORN OR MAY.—Once upon a time, every porch was decorated with a branch of May to avert the evil eye and prevent witchcraft, but the idea has been departed from, and now it is regarded as a harbinger of ill-luck, and is rarely brought inside a house.

THE MISTLETOE.—From very ancient times, this plant has been regarded with curious veneration. Probably it gained special fame, in the first instance, owing to the peculiar manner in which it grew. The Druids looked upon it as a plant possessing marvelous properties, and they esteemed nothing in the world more sacred than it. They gathered it when the moon was just six days old because the moon was then thought to be at its greatest power. This done, they sacrificed two young bullocks which were milk-white. After that, the mistletoe was cut into small pieces with the aid of a golden hook or bill and distributed among the people present. These took it home and suspended it in a prominent place to ward off evil spirits. From these associations, the mistletoe has become an emblem under which young people may kiss, without any evil coming to them through their act.

HOLLY is used as a Christmas decoration because the Romans chose it to hang in their houses on the fast in honor of Saturn. Friends gave bunches of it to those whom they wished to endow with luck and happiness, probably because the prickly leaves symbolized the crown of thorns worn by Christ and the red berries the blood of the cross.

BIRTHDAY FLOWERS

Just as there are birth stones, so there are flowers which stand for each month of the year. By wearing the blossom named for your month, you may count on good fortune as the result.

JANUARY.—The Snowdrop which is the emblem of purity, hope and gentleness.

FEBRUARY.—The Violet, the emblem of modesty, kindness and faith.

MARCH.—The Daffodil, the emblem of daintiness, sincerity and graciousness.

APRIL.—The Primrose, the emblem of lovers.

MAY.—The White Lily, the emblem of purity and sweetness.

JUNE.—The Wild Rose, the emblem of love and loyalty.

JULY.—The Carnation, the emblem of kindly thoughts.

AUGUST.—The White Heather, the emblem of luck and the best of good fortune.

SEPTEMBER.—The Michaelmas Daisy, the emblem of riches and happiness.

OCTOBER.—The Rosemary, the emblem of remembrance and kind thoughts.

NOVEMBER.—The Chrysanthemum, the emblem of faith and truth.

DECEMBER.—The Ivy, the emblem of loyalty, fidelity and faithfulness.

THE LANGUAGE OF FLOWERS

For many generations, certain flowers have been accepted as having definite meanings. Thus, a gift of any of the examples listed below, may be taken to infer whatever description is appended.

CAMELLIA.—Beauty, loveliness.

CANDYTUFT.—Indifference, lack of affection.

CARNATION (Red).—Alas for my poor heart!

CARNATION (White).—Disregard, disdain.

CLOVER (Four-leaved).—Be mine.

COLUMBINE.—Foolishness.

DAISY.—Innocence, purity.

DEADLY NIGHTSHADE.—Falsehood, untrue.

FERN.—You fascinate me.

FORGET-ME-NOT.—The same as the name.

FOXGLOVE.—I bow down to you.

GERANIUM.—To console you.

GOLDEN ROD.—Be on your guard.

HELIOTROPE.—I am devoted to you.

HYACINTH (White).—Your beauty is recognized.

IVY.—Faithfulness. I cling to you.

LILY (White).—Sweetness.

LILY (Yellow).—Gay, happy, joyful.

LILY OF THE VALLEY.—Happiness will return.

MIGNONETTE.—Your qualities are even greater than your charms.

MYRTLE.—Love.

ORANGE BLOSSOM.—Chastity.

PANSY.—Thoughts.

PASSION FLOWER.—Willing to suffer hardships for you.

PEACH BLOSSOM.—I am captivated by you.

PRIMROSE.—A token of love.

ROSE.—A token of love, also.

ROSE (Red).—Bashful, shy.

ROSE (White).—I will be worthy of you.

ROSE (Yellow).—Jealousy.

ROSEBUDS.—A confession of great love.

SWEET PEA.—Leave me and depart, or I leave you.

VERBENA.—Pray for me.

COMBINATIONS OF FLOWERS

In order to convey definite phrases, lovers have long been used to resorting to certain combinations of flowers. A bunch made up of them has the meaning which we print below.

DAISY AND MIGNONETTE.—Your qualities surpass even your great beauty.

FERNS AND LILY OF THE VALLEY.—You are sweet and charming, and you fascinate me.

IVY LEAVES AND YELLOW ROSE.—Your jealousy has put an end to our friendship.

COLUMBINE, DAISY AND LILY.—You have played false and broken our friendship.

PINK AND LAUREL LEAVES.—Your high qualities have been noticed by me.

GOLDEN ROD, SWEET PEA AND FORGET-ME-NOT.—Danger is at hand, be careful. I go away but do not forget me.

SUPERSTITIONS REGARDING ANIMALS

SERPENTS.—These creatures have been regarded from very different angles, according to the time and the country. The story of the serpent in the Garden of Eden has caused many people to detest them: but numerous are the references in histories which go to show that serpents and snakes have been reverenced. In ancient Rome, the serpent was a household god: at other times, it was regarded as a symbol of life and vitality, and it was frequently used as a medium for healing the sick. In India, this creature is looked upon as a mascot for time and wisdom. Thus, it is worn by fanatics as a part of their headgear, and people make metal replicas and wear them as rings, bracelets, etc. Clearly, then, serpents have found more favor than disapproval, and they may be counted as mascots, standing for wisdom, long life and good health.

CATS.—Cats, the most domestic of animals, are regarded with mixed feelings. Generally speaking, they are supposed to be unlucky, though oddly enough a black cat is credited with good qualities when it takes up its abode in a house. This is due to the fact that, during the Middle Ages, black cats were supposed to be associated with witches and in league with the evil one. As a result, people treated them kindly and showered favors on them, not because they liked them, but because they thought that this treatment would avert bad luck.

The person who drowns or kills a cat may look for ill-fortune for nine years. Bad luck attends the vessel or ship on which a cat is found, but on no account may the creature be thrown overboard after the vessel has sailed. This would only make matters worse.

If a cat leaves a house, it is supposed to take the luck with it, and leave nothing but bad fortune behind. If a white cat enters a home, it announces trouble and sickness. A cat licking itself all over signifies fair weather, but if it merely washes its face, it means the approach of rain or storms.

DOGS.—A dog howling under a window indicates death.

Dogs begin in jest and end in earnest.

A dog, a woman, a walnut tree,
    The more you beat 'em, the better they be.

If a dog bark, go in: if a bitch, go out.

A dog will bark ere he bite.

HARES.—If a hare crosses your path, you may look out for a disappointment. If it runs past houses, there will soon be a fire in one of them.

In the Isle of Man, hares are believed to be the spirits of old women, and on that account are shunned as articles of food. In other parts, those who wish to look beautiful for a week make a point of eating hare.

104

BIRDS.—Robins are variously regarded in different parts of the country. Some people think them unlucky, possibly because of their association with the tragedy of the Babes in the Wood. But generally they are welcomed to a garden or house, which is supposed to be all the luckier for their coming. Robins that show signs of being friendly are considered to foretell a hard winter.

Woodpeckers and kingfishers are also lucky, and any suggestion of ill-luck is only possible when birds are deliberately killed after having built their nest and claimed the hospitality of a home.

The screech of a peacock is best unheard when luck is particularly wanted. The feathers of this bird, known to everyone by reason of their beautiful coloring, should never be taken indoors, as they are reckoned specially unlucky.

There is an old superstition regarding the cuckoo. Should a maiden, hearing its notes for the first time that season, kiss her hand to it and say:—

> Cuckoo, cuckoo,
> Tell me true,
> When shall I be married?

she may tell the number of years which will elapse until her wedding by counting the number of times the bird cries "Cuckoo." She must reckon each cry as a year.

Another superstition relating to the cuckoo is that what you are doing when you hear its cries for the first time in any season is what you will spend most time at during the remainder of the year. Folk in the Channel Islands claim that they are sure to be fortunate if they jingle their purses and run a short distance when hearing the cuckoo for the first time in the year.

Owls, crows and magpies do not presage any good: in fact, many people would rather not meet them when anxiety is at hand. An old jingle says of magpies:—

> One for anger,
> Two for mirth;
> Three for a wedding
> Four for a birth.

Ravens are supposed to bring luck to the house where they build their nests, so it is unlucky to kill one.

It is unlucky to touch a yellowhammer in May, since there is the devil's blood in it then.

For a white pigeon to single out a house and hover round it is a sure sign of an early marriage or engagement in that house.

A cock crowing during the night-time means a bad illness for someone close at hand: if it crows during the afternoon, a visitor will arrive.

Sailors are not over-fond of seagulls, believing them to be the spirits of their dead mates, yet they are most indignant if anyone tries to shoot or kill one of them.

OTHER ANIMALS.—A cricket singing within a house ensures good luck for all the household.

Kill a spider and it will surely rain.

See a moth on your clothes and you will get new ones.

A death's head moth indicates bereavement.

Pigs are unlucky creatures when seen singly.

To see a white horse and then, shortly after, a red-haired person, tells of approaching good fortune.

Moles are unlucky to find alive.

Of bees, the following rhyme is prophetic:—

> A swarm of bees in May
> Is worth a load of hay.
> A swarm of bees in June
> Is worth a silver spoon.
> A swarm of bees in July
> Is not worth a fly.

Country people are still given to treating bees as if they belonged to the family. For instance, not a few folk tell the bees of the betrothal, marriage and other outstanding events happening in the home.

PROPHECIES REGARDING ANIMALS

(a) When black snails cross your path
    Black clouds much moisture hath.

(b) When the peacock loudly bawls,
    Soon we'll have both rain and squalls.

(c) When rooks fly sporting high in air,
    It shows that windy storms are near.

(d) Bees will not swarm before a near storm.

(e) When the cuckoo comes to the bare thorn,
    Sell your cow and buy your corn.
    But when she comes to the full bit,
    Sell your corn and buy some sheep.

(f) Little bantams are great at crowing.

(g) Good luck for a grey horse.

(h) Let a horse drink what he will, not when he will.

(i) Trust not a horse's heel, nor a dog's tooth.

(j) Plenty of ladybirds, plenty of hops.

(k) Never offer your hen for sale on a rainy day.

(l) When the glow-worm lights her lamp,
    The air is always damp.

(m) Unlucky to hear the cuckoo sing sitting.
    Or to sit and see the first swallow flitting.

CRYSTAL GAZING

Before we start this chapter, will you just take a look at the following short list of terms used in crystal gazing and spiritualism? You will find that they will make what follows quite clear, and that they will be useful to refer to.

SPIRITUALISTIC.—Belonging to the spirit world.

SECOND SIGHT.—The power which all have (but few develop). The power to see the future and other things with the spirit eye.

AURA.—The circle of thought which each one of us is unconsciously sending out by our characters and personalities.

THE CRYSTAL.—Any object which helps to fix our attention; i.e., a crystal, a bowl of water, shining metal. There is nothing about the crystal that is magical by itself.

PSYCHIC PERSONS.—Persons possessing second sight.

LOOKING INTO THE FUTURE

It is believed that this portion of the book will be found particularly interesting because it is here that we touch upon spiritualism, perhaps one of the most talked-of subjects of today.

In crystal gazing we actually see many things happen which maybe have not happened as yet. In palmistry and astrology we see the signs but not the actual events. Another distinct difference is that in crystal gazing it is impossible to give definite instructions as to how to receive these messages or visions because there is no "how."

What we hope to do in this chapter is to show you that perhaps you possess powers of which you know nothing. Without making the foolish mistake of taking this subject too seriously, you will be able to interest and amuse your friends.

You may say, "But I haven't got this power—I could never see anything in a crystal."

Don't say that, and don't think it! We all have a little of this power sleeping within us. If we wish to improve it, we must use and practise it, but don't overdo the thing.

To understand crystal gazing even a little, it is quite important to know just a few simple facts about spiritualism (the study of the spirit world.) This second sight, or clairvoyance (call it what you will) is merely in its childhood as yet. A very short while ago we should have thought it a miracle for anyone to speak from New York to London along a wire. Now we think no more of it than we should of crossing a road!

So with the crystal. At present a few of us only are able to see, more or less clearly, those visions of the future. Who knows but that in some future time we shall consider this quite an ordinary and natural thing to do, just like telephoning, for instance.

The first thing to get hold of is this: we have not one body but two. An earthly body and its exact copy in a spirit body. By this I do not mean the soul, but rather our earthly body with all its features just as before, is copied in a spirit of ether body. This may sound difficult, but just try to grasp the idea.

In spiritualism there are two of each one of us; one an earthly you, the other (dwelling usually in your earthly body) a spiritual you. But sometimes this spirit body escapes from its earthly prison, maybe during sleep, sometimes when we look into the crystal, and sometimes in what is called a trance or artificial sleep. It is then (when the spirit body is free) that visions of future things are seen, and maybe premonitions (or feelings) of the future are felt.

Our spirit body, with its ten thousand times more clear-sighted eyes, sees things which are invisible to the earthly eyes. This body is able to travel swiftly from place to place, although it always keeps a link or connection with its earthly double.

When a person goes off into a trance, this is what has happened. The earthly body sleeps while the spiritual body roams about the future, past and present, or perhaps visits distant places. It is, of course, able to speak with other spirit bodies, and thus get information about other folk who have "passed over," as the spiritualists call death.

Now perhaps you can better appreciate the wonderful stories which you hear about mediums (people who pass into these trances), who have spoken —or are alleged to have spoken, for the verdict of science is "Not proven"— with the voices of folk long dead, and whom they have never seen.

While everyone does not actively possess this power of releasing his spirit body, we all have it. That this is true can be seen in several ways. Have you never had a presentiment or feeling of evil to come, a strong feeling which it took all your determination and common sense to drive away? Anyway, you will have frequently heard other people saying, "I had a feeling that so-and-so would happen."

That feeling is explained by this wandering of the spirit body; for a short time we have had our spirit eyes freely opened, and have gained a glimpse of the unknown. As our spirit eyes are as yet undeveloped it is but a glimpse, then down falls the thick curtain, and the mystery is once more hidden from us!

Just as some children learn to walk more easily than others, so do some people learn to walk with their spirit body and to speak the spirit language more quickly than others.

Which seems very natural, doesn't it?

Let us briefly refresh our minds with the absolutely necessary facts which you must know to understand the first steps in fortunetelling by the crystal. What we are going to say next will then be more readily understood:—

FIRSTLY.—We have not one body but two, an earthly and a spiritual body.

SECONDLY.—Though normally contained in the earthly body, it is possible for the spirit to escape from its prison, and pass from place to place at a speed greater than light. This occurs during sleep, the artificial or forced sleep of the trance, and also when one gazes into the crystal.

THIRDLY.—We have four eyes. Two earthly eyes, and two very much keener spirit eyes. It is with these spirit eyes that we see the future and the past in the crystal.

FOURTHLY.—Each one of us is sending out thought-waves at this moment. These are known by spiritualists as our aura. It is found in different colors, which depend on our characters or the thoughts leaving us. Certain reds show rage, for instance.

WHAT THE CRYSTAL IS FOR

The first thing to get hold of is that there is nothing magic or in any way wonderful about the crystal itself. It is merely a means of fixing the attention of our earthly eyes, so that we may see the more clearly with our spirit eyes.

Now for a few hints upon actually looking into the crystal.

When you gaze into whatever object you have chosen, your earthly body and earthly eyes pass into a more or less sleepy state, thus enabling your spirit body to escape. That gives us our first point to remember.

Here it is: When you look into the crystal, whatever you do don't worry about whether or not you will see anything! Try to think steadily of what you wish to see; this will at first seem hard, but practice will help you, and practice makes perfect.

Then remember to keep any glare of light from the eyes; it is wise to sit with one's back towards the light. Let your surroundings be quiet and peaceful; there must be absolutely nothing which may catch your attention and so take it off the crystal. If, for instance, a noisy bus or other vehicle were to pass during the time in which you were making your attempt, it would probably disturb things very much.

One should never be discouraged if nothing whatever is seen at the first few attempts. A puppy cannot at first see out of its eyes, and it is the same with a beginner in crystal gazing; his spirit eyes may take some little time to open, while others, more fortunate, may find theirs open almost at once. Never strain the eyes in an unwinking stare. Let them wink and blink quite naturally. To do anything else would be sure to take your attention from the picture which you wish to see.

HOW TO BEGIN

The best thing to do is to try these various methods, and then see for yourself which is the most successful in your own individual case.

Here are a few means you might try, in order to test this for yourself.

Use either a (1) crystal, (2) a polished object, (3) a bright coin, (4) a sparkling gem, or (5) ordinary glass in the shape of a sphere or ball. There are others, but they are not important.

In conclusion, it will be of interest to know just what you may expect to see when, and if, your spirit eyes open. Probably a misty, fogged appearance will first be seen in the crystal. This will remain for some little time, until finally the scene or person (whatever it may be) will appear. The latter may be faint and dim, or it may be clear-cut like a good photograph.

The clearness or otherwise will depend among other things upon the keenness of sight of the spirit eye. It will also be influenced by the degree of quiet, and upon the absence of anything likely to disturb the searcher in the realms of the future.

THE MOON AND THE LUCK IT BRINGS

People of all ages have looked upon the moon as a provider of good and bad luck, and most of us have probably noticed that it has influenced our actions, at times. Here are some of the beliefs that are centuries old.

If you see a new moon over your right shoulder, it means that you will experience good luck all the month.

If you have money in your pocket and you meet the new moon face to face, turn the money over and you will not run short of money that month.

It is unlucky to see the new moon through glass. If you do, go out of doors, curtsey three times to the moon and turn some silver in your hand. This will break the spell which will be cast over you if you do not do as directed. There is one little point, connected with this superstition, which has set us thinking. What of all those individuals who wear glasses? We do not know the answer.

There is a strongly prevalent idea that everything falling to the lot of man when the moon is waxing will increase or prosper; but things decrease and do not prosper when the moon is on the wane.

Irish colleens were wont to drop on their knees when they first caught sight of the new moon, and say, "Oh, moon, leave us as well as you have found us." And, long ago, Yorkshire maidens "did worship the new moon on their bent knees, kneeling upon the earth-cast stone."

If the full moon known as the Harvest Moon appears watery, it is an ill sign for the harvest. (The Harvest Moon is due about the middle of September.)

If the moon shows a silver shield, be not afraid to reap your field: but if she rises haloed round, soon we'll tread on deluged ground.

If the moon changes on a Sunday there will be a flood before the month is out.

A Saturday moon, if it comes once in seven years, comes too soon.

A fog and a small moon bring an easterly wind soon.

> In the waning of the moon,
> Cloudy morning: fair afternoon.
> Pale moon doth rain; red moon doth blow,
> White moon doth neither rain nor snow.
> When the moon's halo is far, the storm is n'ar (near).
> When the moon's halo is n'ar, the storm is far.

It has long been a custom for girls to go to the nearest stile, to turn their back on the first new moon after Midsummer and to chant these verses:

> All hail, new moon, all hail to thee.
> I prithee, good moon, reveal to me,
> This night, who shall my true love be.
> Who he is and what he wears,
> And what he does all months and years.

If she were to be married in the course of the next twelve months, the moon answered her questions during her sleep of the same evening.

In many parts of the country it is supposed that, on Christmas Eve, the moon will help maidens to find out when they are to be married. The plan is for a maiden to borrow a silk handkerchief from a male relation and to take it and a mirror to some sheet of water, while the night is dark. She must go quite alone; but the sheet of water may be an unromantic pail, full to the brim, stationed at the bottom of the garden. As soon as the moon shows itself, the maiden places the flimsy piece of silk in front of her eyes, and, by holding the mirror half towards the moon and half towards the water, it is possible for her to see more than a pair of reflections. The number of reflections are the months which will ensue before her wedding bells ring out.

We recently came across the following information in a document quite three hundred years old:

"The first, second and third days of the moon's age are lucky for buying and selling; the seventh, ninth and eleventh are lucky for engagements and marriage; the sixteenth and twenty-first are not lucky for anything."

The same document affirmed that:

"A baby born before the new moon is twenty-four hours old is sure to be lucky. Anything lost during the second twenty-four hours of the moon's age is sure to be found. All things begun on the fifth twenty-four hours will turn out successfully. A dream experienced on the eighth twenty-four hours must come true."

FORTUNETELLING BY MEANS OF PLAYING CARDS

Telling fortunes, by means of playing cards, is one of the oldest amusements indulged in by civilized people. The ancients of the Far East used their Tarot packs for this purpose long before the birth of Christ, and, ever since, it has been recognized that cards can be made to give a surprisingly accurate reading of future events.

It is interesting to note that, until modern times, it was a common practice of men who had to make great and far-reaching decisions for them to consult a pack of cards and to be guided by what was revealed. Napoleon, it may be recalled, never made an important move unless the cards advised him to take the step. Julius Caesar was another great leader who placed his trust in card readings, and even Shakespeare, the shrewdest of all English writers, shows by a number of passages in his plays that he recognized the use of cards for purposes of divination. As for the noted men and women of today, it is rumored that several derive guidance from their packs when they are in doubt.

Whether the science of cartomancy, the name given to telling fortunes by the aid of cards, is taken seriously or not, there is no doubt that it will afford a good deal of merriment when indulged in by a number of pleasure-seeking friends and relations.

There are few rules governing this science, but those there are must be strictly observed. First, it is absolutely imperative that the person who is consulting the cards should set his or her mind on the matter. Thus, when a definite question is requiring an answer, the question itself must fill the mind. To let the mind wander to outside things or things that are not involved must lessen the psychic effect. Next, every consultant must cut the pack with the left hand, in order to set his or her seal on the order of the cards. Finally, to obtain the most accurate results, it is necessary that the consultant or person seeking the information should shuffle the pack.

THE FOUR-CARD DIVINATION

This method of fortunetelling is some hundreds of years old and references to it can be found in the works of people who wrote in Stuart times. After the consultant has shuffled the pack of fifty-two cards, he or she withdraws one of them at random and notes the suit. The card is, then, put back in the pack, which is again shuffled. Next, it is cut with the left hand, as already suggested.

Now comes the "lay-out." The cards are set face upwards on the table in four rows, each of thirteen. In doing this, it is imperative that all the rows should be commenced at the right-hand end.

That done, the key card is sought. In the case of a lady, the key card is the queen of the suit shown by the card which she picked from the pack at the outset. When it is a man who is seeking his fortune, the key card is the king of the suit indicated by the card he picked originally.

Having found the key card in the lay-out, count nine, eighteen, twenty-seven, thirty-six and forty-five spaces from it, and pick up the cards so placed. Remember that in counting, a line must be always begun from the right; also that it may be necessary to revert to the first or subsequent rows in order to obtain the full set of four cards.

In picking up the four cards, be careful to preserve their order; the first must be set out first, the second must come second, and the same with the third and the fourth. Each card stands for some definite portent, and the four portents supply the reading which affects the consultant.

The portents supplied by each card are as follows:—

Hearts

ACE.—Interests will center more in the home than outside it.

KING.—A person who has the good of others at heart.

QUEEN.—Energy and ability are denoted. There is, however, a strong tendency towards admiration for many members of the opposite sex.

JACK.—Inclined to be selfish and somewhat averse to following the desires of others.

TEN.—A happy marriage is indicated.

NINE.—A somewhat restless nature which soon tires and requires a change of scene.

EIGHT.—This is not a good card for those desiring marriage. If such a ceremony does occur, it will be late in coming.

SEVEN.—There is evidence that an open-air life is what is required.

SIX.—A happy marriage in the near future is heralded.

FIVE.—Happiness will be provided, but it will not be the result of riches.

FOUR.—Marriage is likely, but the measure of affection resulting from it appears to be small.

THREE.—Life will entail many reverses, but a broad mind will conquer them.

TWO.—Marriage will result, but not before many trials have beset the path to happiness.

Diamonds

ACE.—Friendships will spring up where enemies have existed.

KING.—There is a clear indication of social happiness, but the home may be neglected.

QUEEN.—This suggests a strong character, but no great amount of affection is displayed.

JACK.—Amiability is the chief character indicated by this card.

TEN.—There are signs of a large and happy family.

NINE.—There is no need to worry over financial matters; money will flow in when most required.

EIGHT.—The consultant should keep a firm check on bad habits.

SEVEN.—A very upright and high-minded individual.

SIX.—A person who wavers when a decision has to be made.

FIVE.—A somewhat shallow character is indicated, one who takes insufficient thought of the morrow.

FOUR.—The consultant displays too little trust in him or herself. An inferiority complex is possessed.

THREE.—A person of considerable merit, but is shy and retiring.

TWO.—Do not tire of waiting for the good things of life; they will come without any doubt.

Clubs

ACE.—A successful life is ensured in the commercial world for men, and in the home for women.

KING.—The consultant will succeed in whatever he or she most desires, but it may entail a tedious wait.

QUEEN.—There are signs that too high a value is placed on the opinions of others.

JACK.—One who loves recreations and who gives too little attention to the necessary things in life.

TEN.—Expect many trials unless the other cards point to favorable issues.

NINE.—Money affairs will cause a good deal of anxiety.

EIGHT.—There are definite signs that many so-called friends will only flock to you when you can be of use to them.

SEVEN.—You will have your share of sorrows.

SIX.—Divide your life into three equal portions. One will be pleasant, one will be very happy and the other, more or less ordinary. The fates say nothing of the order in which they will come.

FIVE.—You will have few causes for regrets, if you continue as you are acting at present.

FOUR.—There are people who are prepared to damage your reputation. Therefore, be on your guard.

THREE.—If a request is made of you in the near future, be cautious how you reply. Much will depend on the answer.

TWO.—Beware of coming storms.

Spades

ACE.—Much good fortune attends the one who finds this card among the four that are chosen.

KING.—A card which indicates that the consultant revels in doing kind actions.

QUEEN.—This indicates that the consultant is, frankly, a flirt.

JACK.—One who tries to make happiness a feature of his or her surroundings.

TEN.—Fix your thoughts on something devoutly wished for and the Fates will grant it to you.

NINE.—You are given to worrying over things that do not really matter.

EIGHT.—Do not set such store on money. It is not the only thing worth having.

SEVEN.—Be very careful that you do not marry for anything but love.

SIX.—There is every prospect of a comfortable home, surrounded by children who bring you happiness.

FIVE.—Happiness will come to you either early in life or very soon.

FOUR.—You do not know how to handle money and you must be careful that you do not trust it to an unworthy person.

THREE.—You expect too many luxuries. You would be far happier if you valued the simple things of life.

TWO.—Do not be depressed by troubles. They will pass away.

Now that the meaning of all the fifty-two cards is known, one thing more requires to be explained. Let us suppose that the four cards have been drawn from the lay-out, as already directed. It may happen that one of them directly contradicts another card. What happens then? In such a case, the second card to be drawn from the lay-out has the effect of cancelling the first, but the force of the second card is weakened thereby and its portent is lessened. It is because of this that it is highly necessary to remember the order in which the four cards are taken from the lay-out.

THE THREE-CARD DIVINATION

In this case, the first thing is to run through an ordinary pack and separate the court from the non-picture cards. The latter are then shuffled by the person seeking information, who finally cuts them with the left hand. That done, the matching card is sought. The matching card, it must be explained, is a card which matches the consultant. Thus:

(a) A lady with brown hair is matched by the Queen of Clubs. A gentleman, by the King of Clubs.

(b) A lady who is blonde, is matched by the Queen of Hearts. A gentleman by the King of Hearts.

(c) A lady with auburn hair is matched by the Queen of Diamonds. A gentleman, by the King of Diamonds.

(d) A lady with black hair is matched by the Queen of Spades. A gentleman, by the King of Spades.

(e) Grey or white hair is matched according to its original color.

As soon as the matching card is decided on, the consultant shuts his or her eyes, and, with the left hand, picks up a portion of the non-picture card pack. With the right hand, he or she places the matching card on the rest of the pack and the whole is reformed.

Thus, the pack now consists of forty-one cards, forty of them being numeral cards and the remaining one, a picture card. On no account may there be any shuffling at this point.

All is ready. The cards are turned over one at a time, no notice being taken of them until the matching card is reached. Then, the next three cards of the same suit as the matching card are withdrawn from the pack and set out on the table, in the order in which they were found. These three cards provide the reading sought by the consultant.

The interpretations are as follows:

ACE.—You will be lucky in love affairs, if you have not already been so. You will make your partner very happy and your home will be your greatest pride.

TWO.—You are inclined to take life too easily and you are not very keen on hard work.

THREE.—You are a rover and are liable to be very unsettled at times. Remember the old saying that a rolling stone gathers no moss.

FOUR.—You will experience four sorrows in your life that you will never forget.

FIVE.—There is not the slightest doubt that you will accumulate wealth. Probably, some of it will come as a legacy.

SIX.—You will gather many friends around you. All of them will not be of equal worth.

SEVEN.—Your health will be one of your strongest points, unless you neglect it, when it will be sure to rebel.

EIGHT.—You are a fortunate person, and there will be more than one occasion in your life when you will experience a very lucky escape.

NINE.—Do not expect to gain riches by means of games of chance, lotteries, etc. Your fortunes will not be increased by them.

TEN.—You have the habit of looking on the bright side of things. This is a quality worth more than all the gold in the world. Cherish it.

THE MAGIC SQUARE

This is a very old way of divining what the Fates have planned for yourself, your friends and your enemies. The first thing is to take out of the pack all the court cards, as well as the twos, threes, fours, fives and sixes. Thus, all that is left are the cards ranging between the sevens and the tens—sixteen in all.

The second thing is to take your matching card, as described under the previous heading, and to place it with the sixteen cards. These are, then, well shuffled and cut with your left hand.

The next step is to turn over the cards from the pack, one by one, preserving the order carefully, until the matching card is reached. When this is found, the cards that have been turned over are placed at the bottom of the stack that is left in hand and the "lay-out" is commenced.

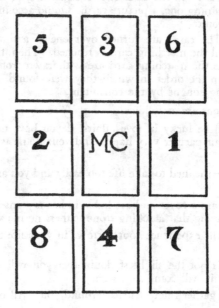

No. 23.—The Magic Square, showing the order in which the cards are to be set out.

The first card in hand is placed on the table and the eight that follow are arranged around it to form a square. This square will thus consist of three rows, each made up of three cards, with the matching card in the center.

It is very important that the eight cards are placed in definite positions, as follows: The first is set down to the right of the matching card; the second to the left of it; the third immediately above it; the fourth just below it; the four remaining cards are placed in the upper left-hand corner of the square, the upper right-hand corner, the lower right-hand corner and the lower left-hand corner, respectively. (See the diagram.)

All these cards are read in the following manner: The three above the matching card refer to the past; the card on either side of it to the present; and the three below it to the future. Next, the three cards on the left-hand side of the matching card refer to your friends; the card above and below the matching card refers to yourself; and those on the right of it to your enemies.

Following this, you must note that a heart stands for very fortunate things, a club for good things, a diamond for things that are passable, and spades for things that are no good at all.

Thus, should a heart come in the middle of the bottom row it shows that you are to be very fortunate in the future; if a diamond fills the same position in the upper row, it is clear that your past was only passably happy; and if a spade comes immediately on the right of the matching card, it is a clear proof that the particular enemy you have in mind is being harassed by a period of ill-luck. And so on, according to which suit fills each of the remaining positions.

THE FORTUNETELLING PYRAMID

A simple way of discovering what kind of luck is awaiting you in the future consists in taking a complete pack of fifty-two cards, shuffling them well, and cutting them with the left hand.

Following this, you place one card on the table, face up. Below it you set out two cards, also face up, and continue with a row of three cards below the two. Other rows follow with four, five, six, seven, eight and nine cards in each, so that the whole forms a pyramid. This accounts for forty-five cards. The surplus of seven are placed on one side when the figure is completed or they may be thrown aside, one at a time, while the figure is being made at any point desired, but it is important that they must be rejected before being seen.

To estimate the amount of luck or good fortune that awaits your future, pick up the last card that was laid down in each row. Naturally, there will now be no card left in the first row, one in the second, two in the third row, and so on until the ninth row will consist of eight cards only. Take the nine cards picked up and sort them into suits. If there are most hearts, you are to be a very lucky person; if there are most clubs, you are to be just lucky; if there are most diamonds you will be passably lucky; but luck will not come your way at all if spades are in the majority.

Should two suits tie for first place the Fates require you to make the pyramid over again.

SEVENS AND THREES

The following method of consulting one's luck must have been attempted many millions of times, but it is not known so well now as it was a century ago. The first thing is to shuffle a full pack thoroughly. This, of course, must be done by the person whose luck is being tested. And then, it is necessary that he or she cuts with the left hand.

After these preliminaries, someone takes the pack and deals the cards one at a time, face downwards, on to the table, placing them in a heap. The consultant who is seeking to find out what the Fates are determining should really be blindfolded, but this is unnecessary if the cards are new and cannot be recognized by any markings on the backs.

The consultant has to choose any three cards as they are being slowly dealt. They can be three cards coming together, or widely separated, or just as he or she fancies.

As each card is selected, it is set aside and, when the three are chosen, not before, they are turned face up and arranged in the order of selection. Each card from one to nine stands for its own value, but tens and all court cards stand for nought. Thus, if the three cards are a seven, a ten and a five, the mystic number derived from them is 705.

The final step is to find out if the mystic number is divisible either by seven or by three. If the total is divisible by either of these numbers, then there is good luck awaiting the consultant; if the total is divisible by both seven and three, the luck is doubled. On the other hand, should there be a remainder when dividing, bad luck is not claimed.

YOUR LUCK IN THE COMING WEEK

A hundred years ago, this method of reading what the Fates were likely to provide for us in the coming week was resorted to in almost every house where a pack of cards existed.

The first step is to pick out your matching card from the pack, as explained under the heading "The Three-Card Divination." This card is set out on the table, face up. Then you shuffle the remainder of the pack and cut it with your left hand. That done, you form a ring round the matching card, using the first seven cards from the pack for the purpose. All the cards in the ring should be face down and none should overlap.

The next thing is to discard the three top cards from what remains of the pack and then to take the third, sixth, ninth, twelfth, fifteenth, eighteenth and twenty-first cards, placing them one each on the seven cards already set out in a circle. These cards must not be looked at while this is being done, and they may be set on the original seven in any order thought fit. But this should be noted, whichever card is paired first must be taken to represent the coming Sunday and the other days follow in a clockwise arrangement.

Thus, the arrangement now consists of a circle, formed of seven heaps each consisting of two cards. Read them thus:

(a) Two hearts in the same heap represent a day of exceedingly good fortune.

(b) One heart and one club, a day of very good fortune.

(c) One heart and one diamond, a day of good fortune.

(d) One heart and one spade, a day of moderate fortunes.

(e) Two clubs, a day as (c).

(f) One club and one diamond, a day as (d).

(g) One club and one spade, a day of fair luck.

(h) Two diamonds, a day neither lucky nor unlucky.

(i) One diamond and one spade, a day much as (h).

(j) Two spades, a day of no luck.

ARE YOU TO BE LUCKY?

Ever since the pack of cards has been constituted as it is now, it has been considered that the four suits have a definite value as far as luck and fortune are concerned. This is a fact that most people probably know, but for the benefit of those who are unaware of it, we will point out that hearts stand for more luck than all the others, that clubs are the next in point of favor, that diamonds come third, and that spades bring no luck at all.

These values are used in the following method of finding out whether you may consider yourself as lucky or not. The full pack is taken and, from it, all the twos, threes, fours, fives and sixes are extracted. These cards are put on one side, as they are not used, and the remainder is shuffled.

The next thing is for you to cut the short pack with the left hand and then to deal it into four equal stacks. Each stack is given one card at a time; that is to say, the eight cards of one stack are not allotted all at once.

This done, you take the third heap, without looking at the other three, and turn up the cards. Most likely all the suits will be represented and the thing is to note how many cards there are of each. If there are most of hearts, your good luck is assured; if clubs predominate, then you are still fortunate; if diamonds head the list, you will have average luck; but when spades are in the majority, your best plan is to tell yourself that there is no such thing as good and bad luck.

One thing more about the reckoning. If, say, hearts occur only four times in the heap, and no other suit is present as often, then, as we say, good luck is yours. But, should hearts occur five, six, seven or eight times, then your good luck is correspondingly increased in amount. The same rule should be applied to the other suits.

PEERING INTO THE FUTURE

You probably have some question that you would like answered. It may concern—well, it can concern anything you like and you need confide to nobody what it is about. This is a method of obtaining the answer to such a question:

If you are of the female sex, take the four queens from a pack and, if you are a male, take the four kings. Place them face down on the table in front

of you and, with your eyes shut, shuffle them round and round, using only
your left hand. Work the cards round in the opposite direction to the movement of the hands of a clock. When you have lost all idea of the identity
of the cards, still with your left hand and with your eyes tightly shut, place
the cards in a line in front of you. Now, open your eyes and turn the cards
face up.

The card to the left of the line stands for "This year"; the card filling the
second position stands for "Next year"; the card coming third, for "Some-
time"; and the card at the right of the line, for "Never." The card that is a
heart answers the question and the others are ignored. Thus, if the heart
fills the second position, the answer is "Next year"; if it comes fourth, the
answer is "Never."

It is claimed by astrologers that a true answer to the question is only obtained on the first occasion that this method is employed after a new moon
has appeared.

WHAT REVERSED CARDS REVEAL

In most cases, the cards of an ordinary pack look the same whether viewed
one way or the other; in other words, if they were cut in halves across the
shortest dimension, each half would be exactly alike. But this is not so in
every case. Take, for instance, the aces of hearts, clubs and spades; with
these the tops and bottoms would be different, though with the ace of
diamonds, they would be the same. All the sevens offer further cases where
the two halves are not identical and the same may be said of some of the
eights. In addition, it must be pointed out that all packs do not follow the
same arrangement, so that a list of these unbalanced cards cannot be given.

Astrologists have long considered that these cards, which are not alike top
and bottom, possess certain powers in deciding one's luck. This is how
they act:

Take a full pack and shuffle it thoroughly, then cut with the left hand.
After that, turn each card over, one by one, and it is advisable to work slowly,
as mistakes are easily made.

Look at every card in turn, count the pips on it that are the right way up
and those that are upside down. When the latter are more in number than
the former, you have a reversed card. Set it aside and continue with the cards
that follow. Note that it is not any card that permits of being reversed, but
only those that are actually reversed, that should be set aside. Note, also,
that a reversed card to you is not reversed to someone sitting opposite you.

When the pack has been run through and all the reversed cards taken out,
note what you have found. Count up the number belonging to each suit.
If hearts are in the majority, you are indeed lucky; if spades figure most, you
are the reverse. Clubs are not quite so lucky as hearts and diamonds rank a
little below clubs.

Should any suit figure much more than the others, then the above readings
are strengthened.

CARD COMBINATIONS

This method of discovering certain facts about your future is as old as the hills, if not older. It depends on laying out the cards and noting how certain of them are arranged.

The first thing you do is to take an ordinary pack and remove from it all the twos, threes, fours, fives and sixes. This will leave you with thirty-two cards in hand. Next, you shuffle very thoroughly and cut with the left hand. That done, you set out the thirty-two cards in four rows, each of eight cards. Be careful to commence each row at the right and then work to the left. Of course, you must put them out in exactly the same order as they come off the pack.

The "lay-out" being completed, you carefully look at the cards. You look, first, to see if by any chance there are four aces touching anywhere. If so, the scrutiny ceases and you find out, from the list given below, what the meaning is of four aces touching. But if there are not four such aces, then you search for four kings and, failing them, four queens, and so on, down to four sevens. If all these fail, you look for three cards of a kind starting as before with aces and working down to sevens. Should there be no groups of threes, then you look for groups of two. Of course, after that there is no point in continuing the scrutiny if there are no twos.

Be careful to understand that the cards forming a group need not all occur in the same horizontal line. As long as one card touches another of the same value, whether at the top, bottom, sides or even at the corners, it will count. Note also that the only reading that may be taken from a "lay-out" is the highest reading. Thus, if there are four aces and three queens, you are not permitted to take the reading of the queens, if you prefer it, to that of the aces. The reading of the aces alone counts.

These are the readings:—

Fours

FOUR ACES.—Dangers may attack you while you are least expecting them.

FOUR KINGS.—You are likely to rise in the world and be endowed with fame.

FOUR QUEENS.—You will be led into quarrels, not of your own seeking.

FOUR JACKS.—Treachery is afoot and you will be the victim, unless you play your cards remarkably well.

FOUR TENS.—You will succeed at what you have most set your heart.

FOUR NINES.—People will endeavor to cheat you. Keep your eyes open and thwart the wrong-doers.

FOUR EIGHTS.—You are likely to form some great desire, and that desire will be attained, if you are true to yourself.

FOUR SEVENS.—There is a very happy home marked out for you, if you wish it.

Threes

THREE ACES.—Good news is coming.

THREE KINGS.—Some great desire that you have is about to be realized. It is nothing to do with work or business, but pleasure.

THREE QUEENS.—You will be happy in one particular friendship that you are about to make.

THREE JACKS.—Certain disputes are trying to find their way into your existence. Be guarded.

THREE TENS.—Wait patiently and a very happy time will not be long in coming.

THREE NINES.—Your wishes may not come true as soon as you would like. But wait.

THREE EIGHTS.—Marriage is imminent for those of single blessedness who have set their hearts on it.

THREE SEVENS.—First, there is a cloud and behind it is bright sunshine. This applies to you.

Twos

TWO ACES.—You are about to start on some new enterprise and make a success of it.

TWO KINGS.—You are shortly meeting a stranger who will mean a good deal to you.

TWO QUEENS.—Doubt is to cloud your mind. You will seek advice from a certain quarter. Take the advice and do not lose sight of the giver.

TWO JACKS.—Your faith is to be sorely tried. See that you do not injure your reputation.

TWO TENS.—There is every sign of good fortune in the future.

TWO NINES.—There is a great surprise in store for you.

TWO EIGHTS.—Be judicious in your dealings with the opposite sex.

TWO SEVENS.—The unengaged are soon to be engaged.

Other Combination of Cards

Should the cards offer none of the above arrangements, the following may be found, but they are meaningless unless all the foregoing have failed.

KING OF CLUBS AND TEN OF HEARTS.—Love is coming.

KING OF DIAMONDS AND TEN OF SPADES.—Beware of lovers' quarrels.

KING AND QUEEN OF SAME SUIT.—A proposal or its equivalent.

QUEEN OF SPADES AND ANY JACK.—Take care of the wiles of a woman well known to you.

TEN OF HEARTS AND NINE OF CLUBS.—A journey is awaiting you.

TEN OF HEARTS AND ACE OF SPADES.—A birth.

NINE OF HEARTS AND ACE OF CLUBS.—Your wishes will be fulfilled.

SEVEN OF HEARTS AND SEVEN OF CLUBS.—Your troubles are about to end.

ZODIAC CARD READING

Perhaps you do not know which is your lucky month. If you would like to find out, the following simple method is helpful.

Take one or two packs of cards, according to the instructions below. Bridge cards are preferable as they are small. Then, cut twelve pieces of paper, each the size of one of the cards. On each piece, draw a sign of the Zodiac and

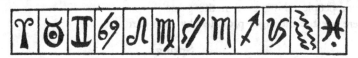

No. 24.—The Arrangement of the Signs for Zodiacal Card Reading.

arrange the pieces on the table, as shown in the diagram. It will be seen that the signs are placed in their monthly order from April to March and not from January to December. This order must be followed.

Next, find out your lucky number, as directed in the chapter "What is your Lucky Number?" For such numbers from one to four, one complete pack is needed; for numbers from five to eight, two packs are necessary. When nine is the lucky number, either use three packs or take two packs and shuffle in with the cards four pieces of paper, each the same size as a card, and on each write a heart, a club, a diamond or a spade.

Shuffle the cards thoroughly and then deal them out, giving each sign of the Zodiac a card in turn. Lay on each sign as many cards as indicated by your lucky number, then stop.

Look at the cards lying on each sign. Wherever you find more hearts than any other suit on a sign, take it as a portent that the month indicated by the sign is a lucky one for you. Of course, it is quite possible and even desirable that you may have more than one fortunate month.

A BIRTHDAY MESSAGE FROM THE CARDS

We have seen this fortunetelling game played at many parties and other gatherings, and it has always caused a good deal of innocent amusement.

First of all, an ordinary pack is taken and the court cards are withdrawn from it. They alone are used, while the numeral cards are put on one side. These court cards are shuffled and the players sit around the table.

One of the players is appointed as the seer. He or she takes the twelve cards, spreads them out in a fan, face down, and the first player selects one. When this card is withdrawn from the fan, it is turned up. While everybody looks at the chosen card, the seer asks the player the date of his or her birth. On hearing the date, the seer notes whether it comes under the heading, spring, summer, autumn or winter. Then he reckons:

(a) Any date in March, April or May as spring.

(b) Any in June, July or August as summer.

(c) Any in September, October or November as autumn.

(d) Any in December, January or February as winter.

Next, he looks down the appropriate section, given below, and reads out the message, according to the card which the player has withdrawn from the fan.

That completes the business for the first player and the performance is gone through afresh, in exactly the same way, for the second and all subsequent people taking part in the game.

Here are the messages provided by each card:

Spring

KING OF HEARTS.—Kindness to an elderly person will result in financial gain to you.

QUEEN OF HEARTS.—A friendship will grow into love, quite unexpectedly.

JACK OF HEARTS.—You are advised not to marry the one that is good looking.

KING OF CLUBS.—You will have a love letter that will cause you some surprise.

QUEEN OF CLUBS.—Show more affection. Coldness is unlikely to bring you happiness.

JACK OF CLUBS.—Money will mean much in your matrimonial affairs.

KING OF DIAMONDS.—The one you look upon as your best friend is a "dark horse."

QUEEN OF DIAMONDS.—You are marked out for fortune's smile.

JACK OF DIAMONDS.—A light-haired woman is anxious to do you a good turn.

KING OF SPADES.—Be very charming to the person with blue eyes.

QUEEN OF SPADES.—You are shortly to come into money.

JACK OF SPADES.—A sudden change in domestic affairs is imminent.

Summer

KING OF HEARTS.—An old acquaintance of whom you have lost sight will return into your life.

QUEEN OF HEARTS.—That for which you have been longing is not far off.

JACK OF HEARTS.—A telephone call will revive some old memories which will please you.

KING OF CLUBS.—Show your love and your love will be returned.

QUEEN OF CLUBS.—A stranger will assist you to good fortune.

JACK OF CLUBS.—You will attend a wedding and something will happen there which will surprise you.

KING OF DIAMONDS.—You are wanted overseas, but do not be in a hurry to accept the invitation.

QUEEN OF DIAMONDS.—You will find happiness most where money abounds.

JACK OF DIAMONDS.—You have remarkable powers which you are not fully using.

KING OF SPADES.—Your happiness lies in marriage. Treat the one who is to be your partner with consideration.

QUEEN OF SPADES.—Live more in the open air and many kinds of happiness will come of it.

JACK OF SPADES.—Be careful to hide your feelings.

Autumn

KING OF HEARTS.—A close relation will share some good luck with you.

QUEEN OF HEARTS.—Friendship will change into love.

JACK OF HEARTS.—Get a move on and your luck will change.

KING OF CLUBS.—Don't let money stand in the way of your marriage.

QUEEN OF CLUBS.—Do not be surprised if an enemy relents and becomes a friend.

JACK OF CLUBS.—Try to forget your disappointment. Happiness is due from quite another quarter.

KING OF DIAMONDS.—Relatives are rising against you. Act fearlessly and they will recognize your sterling qualities.

QUEEN OF DIAMONDS.—You are marked out by the Fates to be the recipient of some very good fortune.

JACK OF DIAMONDS.—Within seventeen days or weeks, a startling offer is to be made to you.

KING OF SPADES.—Make a wish within the next hour and it shall be fulfilled within the next year.

QUEEN OF SPADES.—Avoid the one with the dark complexion.

JACK OF SPADES.—A late marriage will be more prosperous than an early one.

Winter

KING OF HEARTS.—Good friends are ready to help you on the road to success.

QUEEN OF HEARTS.—Do not decide until you are quite certain.

JACK OF HEARTS.—Be cautious of the friends you make while dancing.

KING OF CLUBS.—Get out of the groove you are in and sail away to success.

QUEEN OF CLUBS.—A delightful adventure will pave the way to happiness.

JACK OF CLUBS.—Flirting never gave anybody any lasting happiness. Be more sober.

KING OF DIAMONDS.—Some good news is coming and the postman will bring it.

QUEEN OF DIAMONDS.—Keep your head and you will keep your lover.

JACK OF DIAMONDS.—You have too many strings to your bow and too many irons in the fire.

KING OF SPADES.—You are beloved by someone you least suspect.

QUEEN OF SPADES.—Your affairs will straighten out shortly and then you will understand.

JACK OF SPADES.—Your rival seems to be gaining successes, but wait. In a short space, they will collapse like a pack of cards.

THE WISH CARD

The nine of hearts has long been regarded as the wish card; that is to say, if a player wins this card, in any agreed manner, he or she will have a wish fulfilled.

The most usual way to decide who is to be the lucky individual is for the players to sit around the table and for each to write down a wish on a slip of paper, and then to initial it. That done, the papers are collected and set aside to await the decision of the cards.

The cards are dealt to the players in turn in the ordinary manner from a full pack. Just how many each person is to receive depends on the number of players, but all must have the same number, and each should be given as many as the pack allows. Thus, there will often be a few cards left over. These are set in the middle of the table and not used.

When play starts, somebody begins by turning over the first card on his or her pack. If this is a numeral card, the next person follows by turning over the first card on his or her pack, and so the play continues round the table. But, if someone turns over a jack, the next person must pay that person one card, i.e., the card coming first on his pack. If a queen is turned over, the payment is the next two cards; if it is a king, the next three cards, while an ace requires the payment of the four next cards. The person playing the jack, queen, king or ace takes not only the cards paid but any that may be lying face upwards in front of the person paying. All paid cards are placed at the bottom of the receiver's pack.

There is one point more to note; if, while in the act of paying, the payer turns over a jack, queen, king or ace his debt is cancelled, the previous player gets nothing and the next player has to enter upon the business of paying.

As soon as one player has lost all his or her cards, the game stops and everybody glances through his or her pack to see who possesses the wish card, the nine of hearts. The lucky individual is then given the slip of paper on which his wish is written and must read it out loud. Not until it has been announced to all the company will the Fates take any consideration of it.

OLD MAID

The game known as "Old Maid" is a favorite that will continue to be played as long as cards exist. How it is played is within the knowledge of everybody, but the following variation is not so well-known, and it is certainly more exciting.

Instead of taking out of the pack any of the queens, in this variation the Queen of Clubs is removed. Then, the passing on of cards from one player to another and the pairing, whenever possible, proceeds in the usual way. But a red queen can only be paired with the other red queen, which makes the Queen of Spades a troublesome card.

Whoever is left with it at the end of the game is a very unfortunate old maid, since spades are the most unlucky cards of the whole pack.

THE LAST CARD

Have you some question that you want answered? It may be a question to do with love, marriage, health, finances, or almost anything. Here is a way to find the answer.

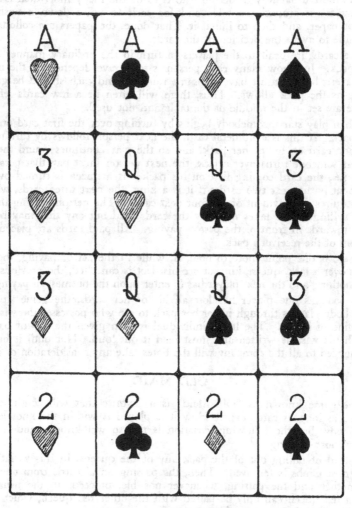

No. 25.—The Last Card.

From a pack of playing cards, take out the four aces, the four twos, the four threes and the four queens—sixteen cards in all. Note that men use the four kings instead of the queens.

Shuffle the sixteen cards and then spread them out on the table, face down. They should lie on the table in a mixed-up heap and not in an orderly pack.

To start, pick any card from the heap, turn it over, and then, according to its value, place it in its proper position, as indicated by the formation shown in the diagram. Suppose, for instance, that it is a two of hearts; then it fills the space of the bottom left-hand corner; or if it is the queen of diamonds, it goes in the second space of the third row.

When the first card is placed, pick at random a second card and put it in the position indicated for it in the diagram. Follow in the same way with all the other cards, from three to fifteen, but not with the sixteenth. This is the card which supplies your answer. If it is the queen (or king) of hearts, your answer will be "Certainly yes"; if it is the two of spades, it is "Certainly not." The other cards come between these two and supply answers varying from "yes" to "no." Their actual meanings are as follows:—

1.—*QUEEN OF HEARTS.*—Certainly yes.

2.—*ACE OF HEARTS.*—Yes.

3.—*THREE OF HEARTS.*—Probably yes.

4.—*TWO OF HEARTS.*—A likelihood of yes.

5.—*QUEEN OF CLUBS.*—It may be yes.

6.—*ACE OF CLUBS.*—It is hopeful.

7.—*THREE OF CLUBS.*—If you are lucky, it will be yes.

8.—*TWO OF CLUBS.*—It is fifty-fifty.

9.—*QUEEN OF DIAMONDS.*—The chances are equal.

10.—*ACE OF DIAMONDS.*—If you are unlucky, it will be no.

11.—*THREE OF DIAMONDS.*—It is not hopeful.

12.—*TWO OF DIAMONDS.*—It may be no.

13.—*QUEEN OF SPADES.*—There is a likelihood of no.

14.—*ACE OF SPADES.*—Probably no.

15.—*THREE OF SPADES.*—No.

16.—*TWO OF SPADES.*—Certainly no.

Be very careful to decide the question before the cards are touched.

MADAME LENORMAND'S METHOD

Madame Lenormand, one of the most celebrated fortunetellers who has ever lived, had a method of divining people's futures by means of cards which we describe here.

20	19	18	17	16
11	7	4	6	10
15	3	1	2	14
13	9	5	8	12
25	24	23	22	21

No. 26.—Madame Lenormand's "Lay-Out."

First, she decided on her client's matching card, in the way explained elsewhere in this chapter, and placed it on the table in the position marked 1, in the diagram.

Next, she took the four aces, twos, threes, fours, fives and sixes from a pack, giving twenty-four cards, and allowed her client to shuffle them, which was followed by the same person cutting them with the left hand.

Then Madame took the cards and arranged them around the matching card in the order shown in the diagram. The layout completed, she looked at the various cards and gathered information from their positions.

It would be impossible for any ordinary person to derive as much information from them as she did, but we can follow the chief lines of her thoughts.

This is how she reasoned:

My client assumes the central position, and around her are positions 2,

3, 4, 5, 6, 7, 8, and 9. Now what cards fill these stations? If there is an abundance of hearts, then friends surround her; if there is an abundance of spades, then enemies encompass her. If there are clubs or diamonds, then just ordinary people are flocking to her side.

It will be seen that Madame gave little consideration to the clubs or diamonds, though she naturally preferred the former, and made her calculations largely on the positions of the hearts and spades. Broadly speaking, the nearer the hearts pressed around the matching card, the better were the fortunes of her client, the farther away were the hearts, the worse were the client's fortunes.

Then, she considered an ace to have a stronger force than a two, and a two a stronger force than a three, and the six weakest of all. Thus an ace of hearts could more than neutralize the evil influences of a six of spades; but an ace of spades would be more than a match for the six of hearts.

We advise you to follow Madame Lenormand's method and see how the cards dispose themselves in your favor.

PATIENCE LUCK

Many people who play games of patience a good deal are convinced that, if they are able to bring three different forms of patience to a successful conclusion on the same day, they only have to wish for something and the wish will be granted to them.

The particular games they play are known as "Tens," "Demon" and "the Idiot's Delight."

It must be understood that there is no necessity to be successful on the first trial of each of the games. Such a thing is almost impossible. What these devotees do is to go on playing until they bring out, say, the "Tens," and then they turn to either of the other two and work at it. Should they be so lucky as to get out all the three, then they formulate their wish and wait for it to come true.

In case some readers do not know how to play these fascinating games, we will proceed to explain them.

TENS.—For this, two full packs are required. The cards are well shuffled and then a row of ten cards is dealt out on the table, face down. This done, another row of ten cards is laid out, also face down. Next, a third row is set out, but this time the cards are placed face up.

The player looks at the ten face cards and throws out any aces. Then he builds up suits, as far as he can, by resting a card of opposite color, and of one degree lower in value, on some other card. Thus, a red goes on a black, a black on a red, a queen on a king, a two on a three, and so on. When the shifting of cards causes a file to have no face card in it, then the uppermost non-face card may be turned over, ready for being used.

As soon as all the possible movements have been effected, a fresh set of ten cards is dealt out, one being placed on each file. The movements are recommenced. Note that not only can one suitable card be placed on another, but partial runs of cards may be so moved, as long as there is no broken sequence in them. Thus, a black two, a red three, a black four and a red five may be lifted in one operation on to a black six; but a red three, a black four, a black five may not be put on a red six. It is possible, however, to lift the red three and black four on to a red five, if such a card is available.

Should a file become quite empty, with not even face-down cards in it, then it is possible to fill it with a king and any proper following sequence, should such a one be within reach in any other file. The use of this movement becomes apparent after a few games have been played.

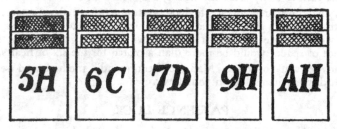

No. 27.—The "Lay-Out" for Tens.

When the second lot of ten face cards has been dealt with, a third ten is set out, and other lots of ten are dealt in the same way, until the double pack, in hand, is exhausted.

The aim of the game is to have no cards left in the lay-out, and this is obtained by building up sequences from "king" to "two" and, as soon as one of these complete sequences is formed, it is removed from the game.

If, when all the two packs have been dealt out and all the possible movements of cards made, there are broken sequences left, then the game has failed and it is finished.

In order to make the explanation absolutely clear, a diagram is given on this and the opposite page. It shows how the cards should be set on the table before any play is commenced. Naturally, the choice of the face cards is arbitrary. This is how the movements will be made:

First, the ace of hearts is thrown aside and the card behind it is turned up. Then, the six of clubs (black) is placed on the seven of diamonds (red) and the five of hearts (red) is put on the six of clubs. The card immediately behind the six and, also, the one behind the five are turned face up. Next, the three of diamonds (red) is put on the four of clubs (black), and the card behind the three is turned up. But the four and the three can go on the five of hearts. So the card below the four is turned. In addition, the cards turned up by the movements of those mentioned may help to continue the sequences.

DEMON.—For this game, one pack of cards is required. After it has been thoroughly shuffled, four cards are placed in line, face up, and then thirteen cards are dealt, face down, in a stack. Some people call this stack the rubbish heap. Next, one card is turned up: it is known as the formation card.

Before any more is done, the four cards placed in line are examined. Should one of them be of the opposite color to another, and of one degree lower in value, it is put on the higher card. Thus, a red ten goes on a black jack and a black queen on a red king, and so on. If at this point, or at any subsequent time in the game, one of the four files, originally formed by the four cards first set down, becomes vacant, then it is filled by taking a card from the rubbish heap.

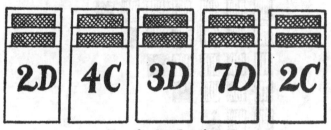

No. 28.—See Opposite.

Now, let us think of the formation card. Naturally, there are three more of the same value in the pack. Whenever any of these three are discovered, they are placed beside the original formation card. The game is to get out the four formation cards and to build up on them in their proper sequence and in the same suit. Any card uncovered in the play, in building up the alternate sequences on the original files, or turned up from the rubbish heap, may be used for the purpose.

When the lay-out has been arranged, the cards in hand are turned over in threes and used for file sequences or formation building. On reaching the end of the pack in hand, it is picked up and turned over in threes again. And this is continued as often as any cards may be used from the pack. When no more cards can be used, there is no point in turning over the threes any more and the game ceases. If the four formation cards have been found and built up with the twelve subsequent cards following them, the game has been successful; but when this is impossible the game has failed.

Note that in a case where the formation card is, say, a six, it is built upon in the following order: seven, eight, nine, ten, jack, queen, king, ace, two, three, four and five.

THE IDIOT'S DELIGHT.—Here, again, one pack is needed. First, a line of nine cards is laid out, face up; followed by a line of eight cards; then one of seven, and others of six, five, four, three, two and one card. This gives the formation shown in the diagram.

The aim of the player is to get out the four aces and to build upon them, in proper order and the same suits, until the kings are reached. If this is managed, the game is a success: if not, a failure.

At the outset, the only cards that can be moved or used in any way are those shown black in the diagram. They are moved according to the following plan: a black six goes on a red seven, a red queen on a black king, and so on. Any number of cards can be placed one on top of the other, if

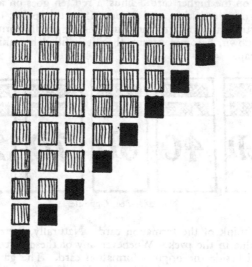

No. 29.—The "Lay-Out" for The Idiot's Delight.

moved one at a time, but it is not allowable to move a stack of two or more cards, except to place it in one of the top nine spaces, and then only when one of these spaces becomes vacant.

Two points remain for explanation:

(1) When one of the cards, shown black in the diagram, is moved, the card above it comes into play and can be moved.

(2) The "lay-out" does not take all the fifty-two cards. There are seven over. These can be used for making up sequences as and when desired.

Now, if you can get these three games to work out successfully and do them the same day, not necessarily the first time you try, frame your wish, a reasonable one, of course, and await the issue with confidence.

FORTUNETELLING GAMES

THE ZODIAC WHEEL

The wheel, illustrated on this page, is divided into a dozen sections, and each contains a symbol that stands for a Sign of the Zodiac. These signs greatly influence our lives. We were born under the rule of one of them, and it is the one that rules our own particular birth-date that we must specially note.

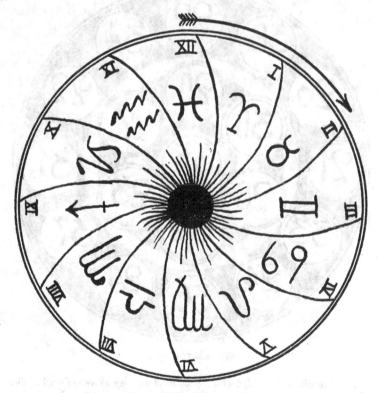

No. 30.—The Zodiac Wheel.

To test *YOUR* luck on almost any question, cut out the wheel and fix it to a wall or door, by forcing a pin through the center. Do this loosely so that the wheel will revolve freely when spun in the direction of the arrow. If it is desired to keep the book intact, copy the wheel on a sheet of stiff paper.

The twelve sections are easily provided with the assistance of a pair of compasses and then the signs must be drawn, as they are done in the illustration.

Before the wheel commences to rotate, blindfold yourself or if you can be sure of playing fairly, merely close your eyes. Then ask the wheel the question about which you desire information, and follow by touching the revolving symbols with some pointed instrument, such as a pencil.

The pencil point will arrest the motion of the wheel and, also, it will touch one of the twelve sections. Be careful to keep the pencil from moving until your eyes are opened. Then, note the section which the pencil indicates.

No. 31.—The Oracle

Take a long pencil, with a point. Place your hand high up above the oracle. Shut your eyes. Rotate the pencil three times and then bring the point down to the paper. Steady the pencil and keep it still: then open your eyes. If the pencil point rests within a circle, the number gives your age when you will be passing through a very lucky period of your life. If you are more than 20 years of age, add the additional years to the number found in the circle.

This is how the wheel answers your question: The reply is "Yes," if the pencil touches your Zodiacal month sign.

The reply is "Probably yes" if the pencil touches one of the sections on either side of your Zodiacal month sign.

The reply is: There is a fair chance of the answer being "yes" if the pencil touches one of the sections two away from your Zodiacal month sign.

The reply is "No" if the pencil touches the section directly opposite to your Zodiacal month sign. Thus VII is opposite to 1, VIII is opposite to II, and so on.

The other sections give no reading at all.

Your Zodiacal month sign can be found from the following table:

I	*Aries*	....Born between March 21 and April 19.
II	*Taurus*	.... " " April 20 and May 20.
III	*Gemini*	.... " " May 21 and June 21.
IV	*Cancer*	.... " " June 22 and July 22.
V	*Leo*	.... " " July 23 and Aug. 21.
VI	*Virgo*	.... " " Aug. 22 and Sept. 22.
VII	*Libra*	.... " " Sept. 23 and Oct. 23.
VIII	*Scorpio*...... ..	.... " " Oct. 24 and Nov. 22.
IX	*Sagittarius*	.... " " Nov. 23 and Dec. 21.
X	*Capricorn*	.... " " Dec. 22 and Jan. 20.
XI	*Aquarius*	.... " " Jan. 21 and Feb. 19.
XII	*Pisces*........ ..	.... " " Feb. 20 and Mar. 20.

Note.—When the wheel is to be spun, the section that corresponds to the date must be placed in the "twelve o'clock" position.

YOUR MARRIAGE MONTH

Here is a very popular game which tells you in which month you should be married. There are two diagrams. The first is a frame, embellished with the signs of the Zodiac. Cut out the blank part in the center. The second diagram consists of two court cards. Cut them out separately, leaving the signs given on the edges. It will be seen that the two court cards fit into the Zodiacal frame.

The game is based on the fact that the signs of the Zodiac are very powerful in watching over people's destinies.

To play this game, place the Zodiacal frame on the table, close your eyes, and twist the frame round three or four times, or until you have no idea of the position of the signs. Then, take the two court cards and, while your eyes are still shut, shuffle them about on the table until you do not know which is which. Pick up either of them, whichever you prefer, but without seeing them, and then proceed to fit the card of your choice in the frame. You will be able to do this by the sense of touch.

When you have set the card in the frame, open your eyes, and examine what you have done. If any sign on the card is immediately opposite the same sign on the frame, it indicates the month in which you are most likely

No. 32.—Your Marriage Month.—The Frame.

No. 33.—Your Marriage Month.—The Court Cards.

to be married. When two signs on the card pair off with two signs on the frame, your choice lies between the two months suggested by the signs. On occasions there will be no signs on the card pairing off with the signs on the frame. These are the instances when the Fates are undecided. The belief is, however, that your marriage month is indicated by a sign on the card being duplicated by the same sign, one position to the right, on the frame. In saying "to the right," the intention is that the move be made in the same direction as the motion of the hands of a clock.

THE DISCS OF FATE

This is an excellent device for those who enjoy fortunetelling schemes. There are four discs and they all have to be cut out. While doing this care must be taken to preserve all the projections intact. Note that the white center of each disc must be removed. This is fairly easy to do if a pointed pencil is pushed carefully through the paper.

When the four shapes are ready for use, slip them on to a long pencil, so near together that they are almost touching. See to it that the disc bearing the lucky devices is fitted on last. It will then hide the three others. The game consists in revolving the discs and, while they are turning, there is a likelihood that they will spread out on the pencil-axis. This can be avoided by slipping a rubber band on to the pencil in front of the discs, and another behind them. Leave just enough space for them to revolve comfortably.

How to Consult the Discs

Place the arrow projections, one at 3 o'clock, another at 6 o'clock, the third at 9 o'clock, and the remaining one at 12 o'clock. When all is ready, twirl your finger three or four times round the disc in the same direction as the hands travel round a clock face.

Then, when the discs have come to rest, look at the cut-out space in the disc bearing the lucky symbols. Count up the numbers shown in this space and consult the lists below. Whatever message is attached to your number, so is your fate. It is well to remember that if any part of a projection comes within the disc-space, its particular number counts, whether it can be seen or not. The fact that the projection is visible is what matters.

You can consult the discs on love, marriage or fortune, but you must decide which you are engaging before the discs are rotated.

Love Answers

1.—Do not be cold. More affection will help on your cause.

2.—Take no thought of interfering relatives. Make up your own mind.

3.—A proposal is not far distant. Give it very careful consideration.

4.—A quarrel, followed by a speedy reconciliation, is predicted.

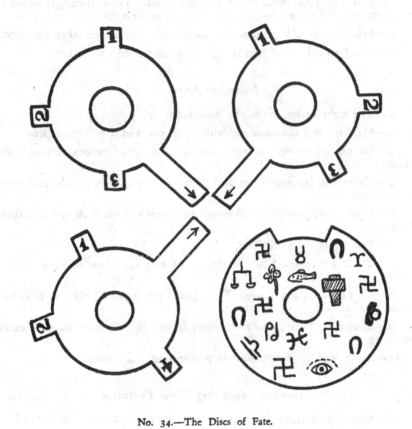

No. 34.—The Discs of Fate.

5.—A misunderstanding will cause a good deal of dissatisfaction; but all's well that ends well.

6.—A pleasant adventure will be experienced by you within the next twelve months.

7.—You are more successful than, apparently, you imagine.

8.—Make up your mind which one you want. There is danger ahead if you keep more than one hanging to your apron strings.

9.—Whatever is to happen will happen soon. Do not be taken unawares.

10.—What you think of him or her, he or she thinks of you.

Marriage Answers

1.—The right person is the one you think.

2.—Marriage will not come suddenly upon you and it will come late.

3.—Do not let money matters enter into the considerations of your marriage.

4.—There will be certain ups and downs to navigate before the ceremony is arranged.

5.—Your marriage will be influenced by a person with dark eyes and dark hair.

6.—You ought not to hesitate.

7. There are as good fish in the sea as ever came out of it, so do not worry.

8.—Do not be in any hurry. Time is not precious and nothing is as important as knowing your own mind.

9.—More than likely, your own wedding will be influenced by some other wedding.

10.—Don't worry. Everything is progressing satisfactorily.

Answers Regarding Your Fortunes

1.—Money will come to you, but not until you have worked hard to gain it.

2.—Expect some important change of position very soon.

3.—Somebody is about to lend you a helping hand.

4.—A large slice of luck will come your way before two moons have run their course.

5.—Do not be afraid to strike out of the old rut.

6.—You are placing too much faith in friends. Be more self-reliant.

7.—When you are least expecting it, you will get all you deserve, and more.

8.—Do not be too keen on experiments. Be thankful for what you already have.

9.—Avoid anything in the nature of "chance" where money is concerned.

10.—You will go on a journey and much benefit will come of it.

THE LUCKY SQUARE

This is a rattling good game for several players. First, give each person a sheet of paper and a pencil. On the paper, a large square has to be drawn, such as is used for crossword puzzles. Each side of the square is divided into six equal portions, and lines are drawn from side to side and from top to bottom. The figure is now a large square, divided into thirty-six small squares—six along any horizontal or vertical row.

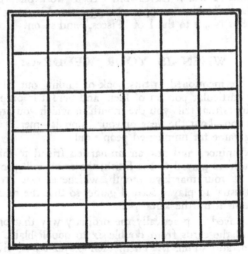

No. 35.—The Square required for this game.

The next thing is to exhibit a card on which is printed the following signs of the Zodiac:

ARIES	*TAURUS*	*GEMINI*
CANCER	*VIRGO*	*LIBRA*
	PISCES	

The card is so placed that the players can see the names and refer to them during the game.

When play starts, the first person chooses any letter he likes, but will probably select one which helps to spell one of the words set out above. He calls out the letter and all the players put it in one of the squares on their paper. That done, the next person selects any letter he chooses, and, on calling it out, all the players put it in another of the squares. The third person does similarly, and so do all the other players, until the game is stopped by someone or until all the thirty-six squares are filled.

The aim of each player is to be the first to spell in consecutive squares, either horizontally or vertically, one of the names of the signs, as given on the card. And, naturally, the aim of the other players is to frustrate their opponents. Obviously, it is forbidden for one person to look at the attempt of another.

The first player to complete a word cries "stop," and if he is adjudged correct, he has a wish granted to him.

There is a good deal of skill needed in this game. Suppose the first competitor selects P as his letter. All the others know he is aiming for "Pisces" and player No. 2 then calls V. Clearly, he is trying for "Virgo." So player No. 3 quietly calls A which leaves him free to work on "Aries," "Cancer," "Taurus" or "Libra." Now, suppose No. 3 is working for "Aries," in calling, say I, he helps No. 1 to the I of "Pisces," and so on.

WHEN IS YOUR WEDDING?

Several ways are mentioned in this book of finding out which month is to bring you some particular portion of luck, and here it is proposed to describe a game of dominoes that tells you the month in which you are to be married. Nothing is told you about the year of your nuptials—merely the month, and it is an amusing game for unmarried people only.

Get out the dominoes and ask an unmarried friend to take a hand with you. When you have played to the finish, the result will provide one of you with the name of your marriage month, whichever was previously decided on. Then, it is usual to play a second game, so that the second of you may receive enlightenment on the same point.

The game is played in practically the ordinary way that one takes a hand at dominoes. All the cards from double-six to double-blank are shot on the table, pips down, and shuffled. Then, each player selects five cards at random and examines them. The player who is seeking information lays down any card he or she chooses and then the game consists in matching the two ends with other cards bearing a number that will match. This is done by the two players in turn.

If at any point in the game one of the players while still holding a card cannot match at either end, he or she must draw cards, one by one, from the heap on the table, until it is possible to match, but one card must always be left in the heap.

The game ceases when one player has disposed of all his or her cards, or when the game is shut (i.e., there are no more cards available that will match seeing that they have all been used) or when neither player can "go" and there is only one card left in the heap.

As soon as the game is finished, the pips at the two ends of the formation are added together, and, whatever the addition happens to be, stands for the number of the month. Thus, if there is a five at one end and a two at the other, this gives an addition of seven, and the seventh month is July. It should be remembered that when a "double" card figures at one end, only the single number is reckoned; thus the total can never exceed twelve, as two sixes, one at either end, is the highest possible score.

It will be very quickly appreciated that the thing to avoid is to stop the game with a blank at both ends. What this means will be perceived by all players.

THE GAME OF LUCK

L stands for Luck, and that is why the track of the game we are now discussing is arranged in the form of this letter.

The game, shown on the next page, is played by two or more persons and the scores are decided by throwing a dice, each person taking a turn.

Should any player arrive at one of the sections marked with a cross, he must go back to the nearest previous station which is a multiple of five; also, if he alights on a section marked with shaded lines, i.e. 15, 50 and 75, he goes forward to the next station which is a multiple of five.

The balloons are so arranged that every player must eventually reach one of them. This is how his luck or fortune is determined:

Whichever balloon is reached, the figures forming it are added up and the key is given below.

100 $= 1 + 0 + 0 = 1$.—You are a favored individual, who should find the world a very pleasant place. You are proud of yourself and your near relations, and you have a reputation amongst your friends that you value. Your worst fault is that you are prone to take yourself a little too seriously.

101 $= 1 + 0 + 1 = 2$.—You have a great deal of imagination and are not slow in recognizing how things will map out in the future. You can turn your hand to a good number of things and are, thus, a useful member of society. Your worst fault is that you are prone to believe too much of what irresponsible people tell you.

102 $= 1 + 0 + 2 = 3$.—You are a hard worker and you are likely to pull your weight in the world. You have an exploring nature and love to go about and see things. Your worst fault is that you are a trifle domineering and like to be obeyed.

103 $= 1 + 0 + 3 = 4$.—You have a facility for calculating and you have a head for business especially if figures play an important part. You are quick in most of the things you do. Your worst faults lie in the direction of grumbling and gossiping.

104 $= 1 + 0 + 4 = 5$.—You have a generous nature and are kindly and affectionate. In most ways, you are a clear thinker, but you have one fault. You are extravagant and must have whatever you desire at the moment, whether you can afford it or not.

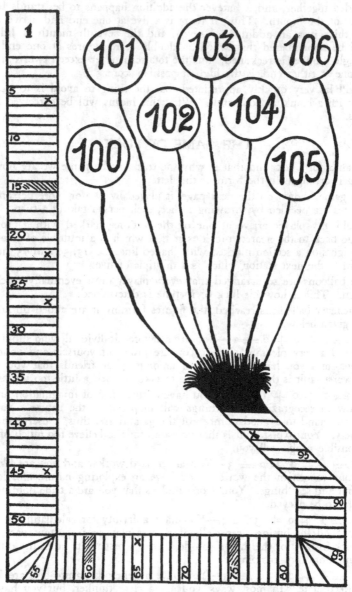

No. 36.—The Game of Luck.

105 = 1 + 0 + 5 = 6.—You have a charming personality, pleasing manners and are entertaining. You are excellent company and make an admirable friend. You will get on in the world, but, even so, you are not fond of hard work.

106 = 1 + 0 + 6 = 7.—You are a careful and patient worker: you are sincere and conscientious; you have an honest desire to get on in the world. Your greatest fault is that you lack a sense of humor and are totally unaware that life has a bright side.

A GAME FOR "GROWN-UP" PARTIES

A good deal of fun can be obtained at "grown-up" parties by giving marks to the various players, according to their merits, as set out in some of the chapters of this book: then finding out who obtains the highest score and adjudging him or her the champion of the evening.

The following details are suggested, but they may be, of course, altered in any way as thought desirable:

PALMISTRY.—First, every player's hand is examined, and the person with the longest Marriage line is awarded five points. Those with shorter lines are given four, three, two, one or no points, according to the length of their Marriage lines.

The same process is then followed in the case of the Heart, Head and Fate lines.

This accounts for a possible total of twenty marks.

..BUMPS.—Second, the players take it in turn to have certain of their bumps read. For this, the chart of phrenology should be consulted and a maximum of five points awarded for the best development of the bumps numbered, on the chart, 2, 5, 6, 7 and 8.

This, also, accounts for a possible total of twenty marks.

HANDWRITING.—Third, everybody is given a pen and paper, and asked to write three or four lines of any passage, taken from a newspaper, in the usual handwriting. Anyone who obviously disguises or distorts his or her writing can be dealt a low mark. When all have finished the papers are examined and assessed according to the hints printed under the heading "Qualities Shown in Handwriting, Alphabetically Arranged."

The writing is tested for the following:

Accuracy, Generosity, Ingenuity, Logic and Wit. As the papers take a little time to check, it is advisable for a helper to attend to them while the next item is progressing.

If five marks are the highest awarded for each test, this will account for a further twenty marks.

THE ORACLE.—Fourth, turn to the Oracle on p. 138, and allow each person to rotate the pencil and strike a number, the eyes being shut during the performance.

Give ten points to the player with the lowest score and deduct one point from ten for each successive score.

This will account for a possible total of ten points.

THE ZODIAC WHEEL.—Fifth, the Zodiac Wheel is set up and each person, before being blindfolded, states the month in which he or she was born, and then asks a question. If the wheel answers "Yes," the player receives ten points; if the reply is "probably yes," then the player is awarded six points; while four points are given for the answer "there is a fair chance."

Here the game may end or it may be continued, at will, by introducing further items. If the program we outline is adhered to, the total of possible marks is eighty.

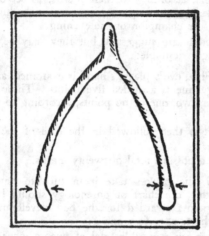

No. 37.—The Wish-Bone of a chicken will provide some good fun. Two rivals hold a tip with two fingers; but their fingers must not grasp higher up the shank than indicated by the arrows. Then they tussle to see who can snap off the larger part of the bone. The winner frames a wish which, of course, is sure to be granted.

THE LUCK OF WEDDINGS AND MARRIAGES

It seems only natural that many superstitions should cluster around a bride and her wedding day, since from the dawn of civilization, if not the birth of humanity, all the world has loved a lover. Every act of hers, according to lore, is fraught with significance and attended by good or evil fortune, and she is hedged round on every hand by customs and conventions as old as the hills.

LUCKY AND UNLUCKY TIMES

The season of the year is an important consideration. She must avoid Lent if she hopes for good luck, but the forty days following Easter are supposed to be extremely fortunate for the celebration of nuptials; and so is June, which takes it name from Juno, the goddess who is generally regarded as the patroness of womankind.

If she values her prospects of happiness, a bride will avoid May. The belief dates from the time of the Romans, who observed the Festival of the Dead at that time. All other religious ceremonies and observances were neglected for the time being, even the temples were closed, and those who contracted matrimony then were considered to be acting in defiance of the Fates, who revenged themselves on the foolhardy mortals. In Scotland the feeling against May marriages dates back to the time of that most fascinating and tragic figure in history, Mary Stuart, who married her third husband, the Earl of Bothwell, then aroused criticism by wearing blue and white, and lived so unhappily all the rest of her life. Superstitious people shook their heads at the temerity of King Alfonso and Princess Ena of Battenberg, who elected to be married on May 31, and were the objects of a dastardly attempt on their lives whilst on their way back to the palace.

WHEN TO MARRY

Marry when the year is new,
Always loving, kind, and true.
When *FEBRUARY* birds do mate
You may wed or dread your fate.
If you wed when *MARCH* winds blow
Joy and sorrow both you'll know.
Marry in *APRIL* when you can—
Joy for maiden and for man.
Marry in the month of *MAY*
You will surely rue the day.
Marry when *JUNE* roses blow
Over land and sea you'll go.

151

They who in *JULY* do wed,
Must labor always for their bread.
Whoever wed in *AUGUST* be
Many a change are sure to see.
Marry in *SEPTEMBER'S* shine
Your living will be rich and fine.
If in *OCTOBER* you do marry
Love will come, but riches tarry.
If you wed in bleak *NOVEMBER,*
Only joy will come, remember.
When *DECEMBER* snows fall fast
Marry and true love will last.

Another poet has given us a different version of the same theme:

Married in January's frost and rime,
Widowed you'll be before your time;
Married in February's sleety weather,
Life you'll tread in tune together;
Married when March winds shrill and roar,
Your home will lie on a foreign shore;
Married 'neath April's changeful skies,
A checkered path before you lies;
Married when bees or May-blooms flit,
Strangers around your board will sit;
Married in queen-rose month of June,
Life will be one long honeymoon;
Married in July's flower-banks' blaze
Bitter-sweet memories in after days;
Married in August's heat and drowse,
Lover and friend in your chosen spouse;
Married in gold September's glow,
Smooth and serene your life will flow;
Married when leaves in October thin,
Toil and hardship for you begin;
Married in veils of November mist,
Fortune your wedding ring has kissed;
When December's snows fall fast
Marry and true love will last.

THE LUCKY WEDDING DAY

Monday for health,
Tuesday for wealth,
Wednesday the best day of all;
Thursday for losses,
Friday for crosses,
Saturday no luck at all.

MARRIAGE DAY SUPERSTITIONS

Superstitions and customs vary greatly in different countries and periods, but they all bear somehow a strong family resemblance.

For instance, one old English proverb runs: "Blest be the bride that the sun shines on," yet in Germany a bride prays for rain, believing that a new joy comes with each raindrop, and that then all her tears will be shed before, and not after, her wedding. There, too, it used to be the custom to take a lot of old dishes to the door of the bride's house and break them to pieces in the street, and if by any chance one escaped, it was accepted as a bad omen.

In China, however, when a marriage was being arranged, and any article of value, such as a vase or a bowl, was broken the ceremony was postponed.

At the wedding feast in Scandinavia someone makes a speech or sings a song, which ends up in a tremendous noise, and this is the signal for a general peal of laughter and for the guests to present their congratulations to the newly-wedded couple.

The Slavs pour a tankard of beer over the bridegroom's horse for luck, and in the North of England, the maid pours a kettle of hot water over the door-step to ensure that another wedding will take place ere long from the same house.

A curious idea among the Burmese is that people born on the same day of the week must not marry, and that if they defy the Fates their union will be marked by much ill-luck.

To prevent these disastrous marriages, every girl carries a record of her birthday in her name, each day of the week having a letter belonging to it, and all children are called by a name that begins with that letter.

In New Guinea it is always Leap Year, for in that island the men consider it to be beneath their dignity to notice women, much less to make overtures of marriage to them. The proposing is left to the women to do. When a New Guinea woman falls in love with a man she sends a piece of string to his sister, or, if he has no sister, to his mother or some other lady relative.

Then the lady who receives the string tells the man that the particular woman is in love with him. No courting, however, follows. If he thinks he would like to wed the woman he meets her alone and they arrange matters.

OMENS OF GOOD OR ILL

There are so many things for good or ill which the bride herself must or must not do that she would have a very anxious time keeping them all in mind if she is very superstitious. These customs begin on the eve of her wedding, when, for luck, she steps on a chair, and then mounts the table to ensure good fortune and a rise in the world.

On the morning of the day—the happy day—if she should be awakened by the singing or chirping of a bird, even of a sparrow, or by swallows sweeping past her lattice at dawn, she may accept these as signs of great good luck. She must be careful, however, not to break anything, particularly the heel of her slipper, as such things spell disagreement and trouble with her new relations.

A cat mewing betokens the same undesirable state of affairs, so she would be wise to see that it has its breakfast in time. If it sneezes, that means the best of luck.

The bride must not gaze on her reflections, however pleasing, in the mirror, after she has fully dressed. If she happens to do so, then she must put another pin in her veil, button her glove, or make some addition to her toilette, to avert evil consequences. The girl who keeps a pin removed from the bridal veil is not supposed to get married, and yet in Brittany the girl who secures one, makes sure of a speedy marriage.

If a small spider is found in the folds of the bridal gown or trousseau, it is accepted as an excellent sign that money will never be wanting in the family, but the spider should not be killed: it must be taken out of doors.

Under no circumstances may the bride read or listen to the reading of the wedding service immediately before the ceremony, not even on the day previous. She must not try on her wedding ring, and if it falls during the ceremony woe betide her. It is considered unlucky to pass a funeral on the way to church, or to meet a monk, a pig, a hare, a lizard or a serpent. On the other hand, it is a happy omen to encounter a lamb or a dove, as both of these are emblems of Christ, and the only forms into which the Evil One cannot enter, according to mediaeval superstition.

A storm of thunder and lightning during the service is regarded as fateful, and so is an open grave in the churchyard. In entering the church and returning to her home or the place where the reception is held, the bride should step with her right foot first. If she sees her groom before he sees her, she will rule him absolutely, but if he forestalls her glance, then he will be the master.

The bride and bridegroom are not supposed to meet each other until they do so at the altar, and in former times a bride did not appear at breakfast, or even emerge from her room, until she was fully attired and ready to go to church.

The forward individual who steals the first kiss before the bridegroom has had a chance to do so is supposed to ensure good luck throughout the year. It was wont to be the prerogative of the clergyman, but it seems a trifle hard on the newly-made husband.

THE ORIGIN OF MARRIAGE CUSTOMS

Since marriage is usually regarded as the chief event of life, for a woman at least, and as most women are highly superstitious, it is not surprising to find that every detail surrounding the auspicious occasion is enveloped in a web of legendary lore.

THE BRIDAL WREATH.—In ancient times in England bride and bridegroom alike wore wreaths conserved specially for their use in church, and in the thirteenth century the bridal chaplet frequently consisted of ears of corn—

signifying plenty. Rosemary was considered lucky in Shakespeare's day. "There's rosemary, that's for remembrance."

ORANGE BLOSSOM.—These spotless blossoms, which betoken purity and innocence, and are symbolical of a prosperous life, are supposed to have been first brought by pilgrims from the Holy Land, and thereby possess a religious significance.

THE BRIDE'S VEIL.—This was originally a fine piece of cloth held over the couple during the ceremony. Later on it was only held over the bride, as it was supposed she was more in need of it than her bridegroom, and so it became part of her attire. In Ireland the old custom still prevails of a sprig of mistletoe, or a twig of hawthorn, being used to keep her veil in place.

THE WEDDING RING.—Since earliest times the giving or exchanging of rings cemented any and every contract. Amongst the early Christians, the thumb and first two fingers typified the Trinity, and the husband placed the ring on his wife's finger in the threefold Holy name. Some authorities believed that the third finger of the left hand was connected by a nerve or artery with the heart, hence its choice for this purpose.

THE BRIDE'S CAKE.—This important part of the wedding feast has come down to us from the Romans, who baked one compounded of flour, salt, and water, which was partaken of by the bridal pair and their friends as they witnessed the wedding contract.

THE BRIDE'S DOWRY.—The phrase "with all my worldly wealth I thee endow" dates back to primitive times when a man bartered so many head of cattle for his bride. This money, known as "dow," or "dower," was originally handed over during the ceremony, and in the course of centuries the bride's father provided its equivalent either in money or kind.

Later still the bride herself spun the linen for her portion, and was not regarded as eligible for wifehood until she had stocked a chest with her handiwork. The term spinster arose in this way, and if a girl's marriage was delayed until she was of mature age she occasionally sold the contents of her linen chest and set aside the proceeds as her dowry. The box, with a lid which is to be found in old-fashioned chests and trunks, was destined as a receptacle for money thus earned and earmarked.

THE GOING AWAY.—The rice and confetti thrown after the newly-wedded couple signifies fruitfulness and plenty, and the flowers, usually roses from which the thorns have been extracted, bestrewing their path denoted happiness, just as the orange blossom and the myrtle of the bridal bouquet were emblems of constancy and never-dying love.

THROWING OLD SHOES.—In Anglo-Saxon marriages the bride's father presented his daughter's shoe to her bridegroom, who touched her on the head with it to remind her that he was now her master. Then the throwing of shoes came to be considered a sign of good luck. "Nowe, for goode lucke caste an olde shoe after mee." The custom, too, is symbolical of the parting of the new life from the old, or of shaking the dust of a place from one's feet and severing all connection with it.

A TEAR HANDKERCHIEF.—In some parts of the Tyrol a beautiful old custom is still observed. When the bride is starting for the church, her mother gives her a fine handkerchief, woven for the purpose of the best linen possible. This is called the "Tear-Kerchief," and with it the girl is supposed to dry the tears she will naturally shed on leaving home.

After the marriage-day the "Tear-Kerchief" is folded up carefully and laid in the linen closet, where it remains till its owner's death; then it is taken out and spread over her face.

THE BRIDAL DRESS

> Something old, something new,
> Something borrowed, something blue.

So runs the ancient rhyme regarding the bride's wedding dress. White is the popular wear, and has been for several centuries, but previously yellow, pink, and a brilliant scarlet were frequently chosen, unless by a girl named Mary, who was expected to wear blue, the Virgin's sacred color. Some years ago, the daughter of a duke, who was united in marriage to a commoner, shocked society by insisting on a "green" wedding. In less than a year, she and her baby were buried in the family tomb.

WHICH COLOR

> Married in white, you have chosen aright.
> Married in green, ashamed to be seen.
> Married in grey, you will go far away.
> Married in red, you will wish yourself dead.
> Married in blue, love ever true.
> Married in yellow, ashamed of your fellow.
> Married in black, you will wish yourself back.
> Married in pink, your spirits will sink.
> Married in brown, you'll live out of town.
> Married in pearl, you'll live in a whirl.

THE BRIDEGROOM

The groom, as the secondary figure in the day's ceremonies, escapes very easily as far as superstition goes, and may do pretty well what he pleases, save letting his hat or the ring drop, both of which are very unlucky. He should carry a tiny horseshoe in his pocket, and fee the clergyman with an odd sum of money.

No one ought to hand him or his bride a telegram on the way to church, and if he wishes to be master in his own house, then he must take care to see her before she has time to catch a glimpse of him ere arriving at the altar.

MARRIAGE PROVERBS

Happy is the wooing that's not long in doing.

Marrying for love is risky, but God smiles on it.

The married man must turn his staff into a stake.

> Mary in May, rue for aye.
> Marry in Lent, live to repent.

Advent marriage doth deny, but Hilary gives thee liberty: Septuagesima says thee nay, eight days from Easter says you may: Rogation bids thee to contain, but Trinity sets thee free again.

Happy is the bride that the sun shines on.

My son's my son till he gets him a wife.

To change the name and not the letter is to change for the worse and not the better.

Wedlock's a padlock.

He who marrieth does well; but he who refrains from marriage doth better.

> Needles and pins; needles and pins,
> When a man marries, his trouble begins.

> Honest men marry soon,
> Wise men not at all.

Marry in haste: repent at leisure.

He who repents him not of his marriage, sleeping and waking, in a year and a day, may lawfully go to Dunmow and fetch a gammon of bacon.

It will not always be a honeymoon.

Keep your eyes wide open before marriage and half shut afterwards.

Lips, however rosy, need feeding.

Marriage with peace is the world's paradise: with strife, this life's purgatory.

Marry above your match, and you get a good master.

Marry for love and work for silver.

Marriages are made in heaven.

Don't marry for money, but seek where money is.

A man may not wive, and also thrive all in the same year.

Better be half hanged than ill wed.

He that marries for wealth sells his liberty.

He that marries late, marries ill.

He that is needy when he is married shall be rich when he is buried.

Better have an old man to humor than a young rake to break your heart.

Marry your sons when they will; your daughters when you can.

Marry your daughters betimes, lest they marry themselves.

Two heads are better than one, or why do folks marry?

FOLKLORE AND SUPERSTITIONS OF THE MONTHS

JANUARY

This month is so called in honor of the god Janus, who is always depicted with two faces or heads, one to look forwards, the other backwards. His work was to preside over the beginning of any new thing and, ever since his time, people have invoked his aid and sympathy when they have been setting out on some new enterprise. On New Year's Day, the Romans gave presents to one another, much as we do at Christmas, but accompanying the gifts was usually a small copper token showing the double head of Janus. To possess one of these tokens ensured prosperity when commencing some new work, and it was supposed to carry enterprises already started, but not yet finished, to a successful conclusion. The accompanying illustration gives a reproduction of one of the tokens used.

No. 38.—Janus, the Two-Headed God. On New Year's Day the Romans gave copper medallions bearing this device to their friends. To possess such a medallion was a sure way to be lucky in commencing any new piece of work or any new enterprise.

NEW YEAR SUPERSTITIONS.—Endless are the superstitions which have gathered around the dawn of the New Year, which, although neither a Christian nor a Church festival, afford sober reflection to many. In several districts, the custom known as "first-footing" is still common. People wait until the old year has been rung out and then they call on their friends to wish them a happy new year. They must not go empty-handed, however, or this will provide a lean year for the friends. A cake will ensure abundance, a red herring stands for luck, and the gift of even the smallest coin is a certain portent that a lucky financial year is opening.

While anyone is free to pay these visits, it is much the happiest omen if the caller be a man, a dark-haired man, and if he takes with him a lump of coal and a fish. Any fish serves the purpose—even a tin of sardines. Let a man, answering these requisites, be the first to cross the threshold of your door, after the old year has gone, and there is no better way of entering on the new year.

Another custom, which has many supporters, is to tidy up the house, to build up the fires and to open wide the front door, just when the old year is departing. The open door allows the exhausted year to make its exit completely. It is then supposed to take with it anything savoring of ill-fortune. The tidy house welcomes the new year in a spirit of brightness and gladness.

For a clock to stop just as the new year is coming in, or to be found to have stopped then, is an ill omen. Therefore, householders have long been careful to give an eye to their timepieces some little while before.

Weather-lore regarding the new year is plentiful. Here is a well-known rhyme:

> If on New Year's night wind blow south,
> It betokeneth warmth and growth:
> If west, much milk and fish in the sea:
> If north, much cold and snow there will be:
> If east, the trees will bear much fruit:
> If north-east, flee it, man and brute.

January has been described as follows:

> The blackest month in all the year
>   Is the month of Janiveer.
> In Janiveer, if the sun appear,
>   March and April will pay full dear.
> If January calends be summerly gay,
>   It will be winterly weather till the calends of May.

(The calends, it may be explained, were the first days of the months.)

ST. PAUL'S DAY (January 25th)

> If St. Paul's Day be faire and cleare,
>   It doth betide a happy year:
> But if by chance it then should rain,
>   It will make deare all kinds of graine:

> And if ye clouds make dark ye sky,
>   Then meate and fowles this year shall die:
> If blustering winds do blow aloft,
>   Then wars shall trouble ye realm full oft.

FEBRUARY

February derives its name from Februare—to expiate, to purify. In this connection, it is interesting to note that on the 2nd of the month falls Candlemas Day, which is the purification of the Blessed Virgin Mary.

CANDLEMAS DAY (February 2nd)

(a) If Candlemas Day be fair and bright,
Winter will have another flight:
But if Candlemas Day brings clouds and rain,
Winter is gone and won't come again.

(b) If Candlemas Day be fine and clear,
Corn and fruits will then be dear.
(There'll be twa winters in the year.)

ST. VALENTINE'S DAY (February 14th).—Like so many of our old observances, the festival of St. Valentine dates from the time of the Romans, but the Church rechristened the custom and called it after one or two saints of the name, both of whom were martyred, one in the third and the other in the fourth century.

Latterly, the day has been dedicated to Cupid by fond lovers who believe it to be the date on which each bird chooses its mate.

The poet Drayton sings:—

Each little bird this tide
Doth choose her loved peer,
Which constantly abide
In wedlock all the year.

Charms and omens are in favor on St. Valentine's Eve. Maidens decorate their pillows with five bay leaves and firmly believe that, if they dream of their lover then, they will be married to him in the course of the year. Another fancy is that the first person of the opposite sex whom one encounters, that morning is destined to be one's husband or wife. Naturally, there must be some sort of friendship in view previously.

A weather prophecy regarding February runs:—

All the months in the year
Curse a fair Februeer.
February fill the dyke,
Weather, either black or white.
If February gives much snow,
A fine summer it doth foreshow.

In Cornwall, there is a proverb, "A February spring is not worth a pin," and the same thought is expressed in Wales by the saying that "The Welshman had rather see his dam on the bier than to see a fair Februeer."

MARCH

March was given its name by the Romans in honor of Mars, the God of War, as at this time of the year the weather was such that it enabled them to begin their campaigns after the worst of the winter was over. The Saxons called this month *LENET MONAT*, meaning "length month," in reference to the lengthening of the days.

Several weather prophecies refer to March:—

(a) A peck of March dust and a shower in May
     Make the corn green and the fields gay.

(b) As many mists in March you see,
     So many frosts in May will be.

(c) A peck of March dust is worth a king's ransom.

(d) March damp and warm
     Will do farmers much harm.

(e) Eat leeks in March and garlic in May,
     And all the year after physicians may play.

(f) March search, April try,
     May will prove whether you live or die.

(g) If on St. Mary's Day (March 25th) it's bright and clear
     Fertile 'tis said will be the year.

(h) A dry and cold March never begs its bread.

(i) A frosty winter, a dusty March, a rain about Averil, another
     about the Lammas time (Aug. 1st), when the corn begins
     to fill, is worth a plough of gold.

(j) March flowers make no summer bowers.

(k) March winds and April showers bring forth May flowers.

(l) Whatever March does not want, April brings along.

(m) On Shrove Tuesday night, though thy supper be fat,
     Before Easter Day thou mayst fast for all that.

APRIL

The word April is probably derived from the Latin, *Aperio*, I open, since spring generally begins and Nature unfolds her buds in this month.

April is regarded as the most sacred month in the calendar of the Church, since it usually includes Good Friday, on which day blacksmiths once refused to work owing to the fact that one son of Vulcan made the nails for the Crucifixion.

FIRST OF APRIL.—The great majority of the old-time customs which clustered round this day and contributed a dash of gaiety and humor to the more prosaic, everyday life of the community, have fallen into the limbo of forgotten things, and the day is chiefly remembered by schoolchildren, who exercise their juvenile ingenuity in playing pranks on their fellows.

The most careful research has failed to ascertain the exact origin of these observances, and someone has hazarded the theory that they began with the advent of the second man on earth, who sought to try the effects of a practical joke on the first.

Anyhow, a form of fooling may be traced to the time of the Roman Empire, but little mention of such a thing is to be found in English literature until the eighteenth century, although "Hunting the Gowk," the sending of some half-witted youth, the village idiot, on some utterly absurd errand from house to house, was long before then a favorite pastime in Scotland, and in France, too.

A weather prophecy for this day runs:

> If it thunders on All Fools Day,
> It brings good crops of corn and hay.

SIMNEL OR MOTHERING SUNDAY.—It is a very old custom to make rich cakes during Lent and Easter, which are known as Simnel cakes. In South Lancashire the fourth Sunday of Lent is known as Simnel or Mothering Sunday, and young people provide themselves with delicious cakes "'gainst they go a-mothering." The sons and daughters present these to their mothers, who in turn regale their families with "furmenty" or "frumenty," derived from froment (wheat), as the dish was made of wheat and milk, with the addition of a few raisins. For children to fail in paying this compliment to their mothers is sometimes taken as a sign that they will have no further opportunity of doing so.

GOOD FRIDAY.—It is a misnomer to name the world's blackest Friday thus, but the words are a corruption of *GOD'S FRIDAY*. Many quaint and curious customs are connected with its celebration, the origins of which are not merely secular but pagan, as well.

For instance, the worship of Terminus, the Romans' pagan god, has still left its mark on Christian England, where, in certain parishes, the custom known as "beating the bounds" is still kept up. Terminus decreed that everyone possessing land should mark the boundaries with stones and pay honor to Jupiter once a year. Failure to do this would invoke the wrath of Jupiter and the crops growing on the land would be blighted. Good Friday or the days previous were marked out for the ceremony.

A wet Good Friday has always been considered favorable for crops, although people on pleasure bent will think otherwise:

"A wet Good Friday and a wet Easter Day foreshows a fruitful year."

It may be useful to add here a saying about the day previous to Good Friday; it runs, "Fine on Holy Thursday, wet on Whit-Monday. Fine on Whit-Monday, wet on Holy Thursday."

HOT-CROSS BUNS.—Hot-cross buns may be either a survival of the sacred cakes offered in the temples to the gods, or of the unleavened bread eaten by the Jews at the Passover. Bread marked with crosses was common in ancient Egypt before the days of Christianity. It is an old belief that the eating of buns on this day protects the house from fire, and other virtues are ascribed to them. For instance, to eat such a bun grants a wish that you may be anxious to realize.

EASTER.—This name is derived from *Eoster,* the goddess of light and of spring, in whose honor a festival was held in the month of April. Few, if any of the old customs observed at this time still survive.

Eggs, as being the emblem of the Resurrection, are peculiar to the feast of Easter, and it is lucky to eat them on the morning of Easter Sunday. At one time, paschal candles were lit to signify the Resurrection of our Lord. These were of colossal size, and each church seemed to vie with its neighbor as to which should have the largest. Easter Sunday was known as Joy Sunday, and was celebrated by gifts to the poor and the liberation of prisoners. It was a time when all differences of opinion should be swept aside and enemies should be forgiven. To harbor enmity against others was to ensure a time of blackness for oneself.

Many curious customs used to be observed. Most of them have fallen into decay, but in some parts of the country bouquets in the form of balls are still presented, and graves are decorated with sweet spring flowers.

Weather observances are numerous:—

(a) April weather.
   Rain and sunshine both together.

(b) If the first three days in April be foggy,
   Rain in June will make the lanes boggy.

(c) If Christmas is snow, Easter is mud.

(d) If Easter is late, there will be a long, cold spring.

(e) A dry April, not the farmer's will.
   April wet is what he would get.

(f) When April blows his horn (i.e., thunders),
   It's good for hay and corn.

MAY

Some authorities maintain that the month takes its name from Maia, the mother of the god Hermes or Mercury; others claim that it comes from Majores or Maiores, the Senate of the first constitution of Rome.

WHITSUNTIDE.—Whitsuntide, which shares pride of place in the Church Calendar with Christmas and Easter, is closely connected with the Jewish feast of Pentecost, which became identified with one of the great summer festivals of the pagan inhabitants of Western Europe, and this idea is borne out by the fact that Whitsuntide has always been the most popular festival period of the year.

It was commonly celebrated in all parts of the country by what was termed Whitsun ale, which was usually consumed under the auspices of the churchwardens in some barn near the church, when all assembled agreed to be good friends for once in the year and spend the day in "sober" joy.

The day was a prolonged picnic, for each parishioner brought what victuals he could spare. The squire and his lady came with their pipe and taborer, the young folk danced or played at bowls, and the old looked on while they sipped their ale, which was brewed fairly strong for the occasion and sold by the churchwardens for the repairs of the church.

During the Middle Ages, Whitsun services were marked by some curious customs, one of which was the letting down of a dove from the roof, another the dropping of balls of fire, of rose leaves, and the like.

THE MORRIS DANCES.—Whitsuntide was pre-eminently the time for the performance of the Morris dances, which some suppose derive their name from the Spanish Moriseo, a Moor, and the dance was originally identified with the fandango. Others believed them to be connected with one of the season's pagan observances prevalent amongst primitive communities and associated in some mysterious manner with the fertilization and slaughter of all living things.

Usually the Morris dances were only performed at special seasons once or twice a year, and in some districts they were only indulged in at Christmas. It is highly significant, and bears out the belief in the religious origin of the movement, that the first of the Whitsuntide dances in some villages was performed on the top of the tower of the church. Lucky indeed were those who took part in these church-top revels, for they were certain to be free of the devil's attentions for some while to come.

Weather lore affirms the following:—

(a) Dry May
    Brings nothing gay.

(b) Mist in May, heat in June,
    Makes the harvest come right soon.

(c) Shear your sheep in May,
    And shear them all away.

(d) Change not a clout
    Till May be out.

(e) A dry May and a leaking June
    Make the farmer whistle a merry tune.

(f) A May wet was never kind yet.

(g) For an east wind in May,
    'Tis your duty to pray.

(h) Fogs in February mean frosts in May.

(i) Who shears his sheep before St. Gervatius' Day
(May 13th), loves more his wool than his sheep.

JUNE

June owes its name to Juno, the goddess of heaven, who takes a special interest in women and protects their interests. She is supposed to accompany every woman through life, from the moment of her birth to her death. Little wonder, then, that the women of ancient times considered that, by propitiating Juno, their fortunes were assured. This they usually did on their birthdays.

Midsummer Day (June 24th) is sacred to the memory of John the Baptist, and the ceremonies practised at this season in the Middle Ages were partly relics of the saints and partly relics of old sun worship. Great fires of wood or bones blazed on every mountain top, and were supposed to be typical of the saint, who was called a burning and a shining light.

These Beltane fires burned often on bare, flat rocks, not only in England, Scotland, and Ireland, but on the Alps, the Hartz Mountains, and elsewhere. It was a great thing to be present at or in view of one of these fires, for the evil spirit was dispelled by the potency of the light and flames.

Rhymes regarding June:—

(a) A dripping June
Brings all things in tune.

(b) If St. Vitus' Day (June 14th) be rainy weather,
It will rain for thirty days together.

(c) He who bathes in May will soon be laid in clay;
He who bathes in June will sing a merry tune;
But he who bathes in July will dance like a fly.

(d) Look at your corn in May,
And you will come weeping away:
Look at the same in June,
And you'll sing a merry tune.

(e) June, damp and warm, does the farmer no harm.

(f) If it rains on Midsummer Eve, the filberts will be spoilt.

JULY

This month was so named in honor of Julius Caesar, whose birth-month it was. The Saxons called it Hey Monat on account of the hay harvest.

The following old sayings regarding July may be noted with interest:—

(a) A shower of rain in July,
When the corn begins to fill
Is worth a plough of oxen
And all belonging theretill.

(b) Ne'er trust a July sky.

(c) Whatever July and August do not boil, September cannot fry.

(d) If the first of July it be rainy weather,
    It will rain more or less for four weeks together.

(e) Dog days bright and clear
    Indicate a happy year.
    But when accompanied by rain,
    For better times our hopes are vain.
    (The dog days are from July 3rd to Aug. 11th.)

(f) St. Swithin's Day, if ye do rain,
    For forty days it will remain.
    St. Swithin's Day an ye be fair,
    For forty days 'twill rain nae mair.
    (St. Swithin's Day is July 15th.)

(h) Whoever eats oysters on St. James's Day will never want
    money. (July 25th.)

AUGUST

Augustus Caesar, not to be behind Julius, named this month in honor
of himself. He was born in September, and it may seem strange that he did
not bestow his name on that month; but he preferred August as a number
of lucky incidents befell him then, and he gained several important victories.

Rhyming prophecies regarding this month are as follows:—

(a) If Bartlemy's Day (Aug. 24th) be fair and clear,
    Hope for a prosperous autumn that year.

(b) Dry August and warm,
    Doth harvest no harm.

(c) Yet there is a saying that "A wet August never brings dearth."

(d) On St. Mary's Day (Aug. 15th) sunshine
    Brings much good wine.

(e) So many August fogs,
    So many winter mists.

(f) Mud in May means bread in August.

(g) After Lammas (Aug. 1st) the corn ripens as much by
    night as by day.

(h) As the Dog days commence, so they end.
    (The Dog days are from July 3rd to Aug. 11th.)

(i) All the tears that St. Swithin can cry;
    St. Bartlemy's dusty mantle wipes dry.
    (St. Swithin's Day is July 15th, and St. Bartlemy's
    Day Aug. 24th.)

SEPTEMBER

September takes its name from the Latin word, *septem*, meaning seven. It was the seventh month of the year as long as March was constituted the first month. The Saxons named it Gerst Monat, or barley month, because they reaped the barley then.

Sayings regarding the month:—

(a) If it be fair on the First, it will be fair all the month.

(b) A wet June makes a dry September.

(c) September blow soft,
Until the fruit is in the loft.

(d) If Matthew's Day (Sept. 21st) is bright and clear
There will be good wine in the coming year.

(e) If the hart and the hind meet dry and part dry on Rood Day
Fair (Sept. 14th), for six weeks there will be no more rain.

(f) If on September 19th there is a storm from the south, a mild
winter is certain.

(g) If it does not rain on St. Michael's (Sept. 29th) and Gallus
(Oct. 16th), a dry spring is certain for the coming year.

(h) If St. Michael's (Sept. 29th) brings many acorns, Christmas will
cover the fields with snow.

(i) So many days old the moon on Michaelmas Day (Sept. 29th), so
many floods after.

(j) Michaelmas chickens and parsons' daughters never come to good.

OCTOBER

October is so called from being the eighth month in the old Latin calendar.

ALL HALLOW E'EN.—Hallow E'en, the vigil of All Saints' Day, was wont to be a season of merry gathering and quaint observances, especially where lovers were concerned. It is still kept up with great success in Scotland. Propitious omens were sought. Nuts, for instance, were burnt in pairs. If they lay still and burned together, it meant a happy marriage, but if they flew apart, the lovers would not live in harmony. All sorts of charms were practised. Girls pared apples and sought to discern an initial in the shape the peel assumed. The apple had to be peeled in one strip without any break, and the whole strip was then thrown over the left shoulder. Also, they stuck an apple pip on each cheek, and that which fell off first indicated that the love of him whose name it bore was unsound.

The customs varied with the locality, but many of them were not unlike the rites of St. Valentine's Day. Burns's poem enshrined most of the Scottish practices, such as throwing a ball of blue yarn into a kiln, winding it in a new one off the old, and, as the end was approached, the maiden enquired, "Who holds?" and a voice from the kiln-pot gave her the name of her future spouse.

Some girls took a candle into a dark room and peered into a looking glass while they ate an apple or combed their hair, and saw the face of their true love looking over their shoulder. Others went out into the garden in couples, hand in hand, with eyes shut, and pulled the first kail-runt or plant they came to. According to its being big or little, straight or crooked, it was regarded as prophetic of the kind of man they would marry. If the heart of the stem was soft or hard, so would be the man's nature, and, if any earth adhered to the root, it signified "tocher" or fortune.

October prophecies:—

(a) If October brings much frost and wind,
Then are January and February mild.

(b) Dry your barley in October and you will always be sober.

(c) In October manure your field,
And your land its wealth shall yield.

(d) October never has more than fifteen fine days.

NOVEMBER

November was the ninth month according to the old Latin calendar. It was known as Wint Monat, or wind month, by the Saxons, as the stormy weather then experienced prevented the Vikings putting to sea and attacking their shores. It was sometimes called Blot Monat, or blood month, as it was then customary to kill large numbers of cattle and salt them for winter use.

November prophecies:

(a) If ducks do slide at Hollantide (Nov. 11th),
At Christmas they will swim.
If ducks do swim at Hollantide,
At Christmas they will slide.

(b) At St. Martin's Day (Nov. 11th),
Winter is on the way.

(c) Set trees at Allhallo'n-tide (Nov. 1st), and command them to grow. Set them at Candlemas (Feb. 2nd) and beg them to prosper.

(d) Where the wind is on Martinmas Eve. (Nov. 10th), there it will be for the rest of the winter.

(e) If there be ice that will bear a duck before Martinmas (Nov. 11th), there will be none that will bear a goose all the winter.

(f) Wind north-west at Martinmas (Nov. 11th), severe winter to come.

(g) As at Catherine (Nov. 25th), foul or fair, so will be the next February.

DECEMBER

Decem means ten and December was the tenth month of the early Roman calendar. Probably it has had more names conferred upon it than any other of the twelve months. Among the Saxons, it was originally Winter Monat, but after their conversion to Christianity, it was Heligh Monat, or holy month, in honor of the birth of Christ.

December proverbs:

(a) December frost and January flood,
Never boded the husbandman good.

(b) Frost on the shortest day (Dec. 22nd) indicates a severe winter.

(c) The day of St. Thomas, the blessed divine

Is good for brewing, baking and killing fat swine.
(St. Thomas's Day is Dec. 21st.)

(d) Never rued the man that laid in his fuel before St. John (Dec. 27).

CHRISTMAS EVE.—The Latin Church called Christmas the Feast of Lights, because Christ, the true light, had come into the world, hence the Christmas candle and the Yule log, which sometimes were of immense size.

"Now blocks to cleave this time requires,
'Gainst Christmas for to make good fires."

In the western parts of Devonshire, a superstitious notion prevails that on Christmas Eve at 12 o'clock the oxen in the stalls are found on their knees, as in an attitude of devotion.

Mince pies were intended to represent the offerings of the wise men. As many of the ingredients come from the East, the connection of ideas is plain, but what can be the origin of the notion that it is desirable to eat mince pies made by as many different cooks as possible to ensure as many happy months is not so easily explained. Some authorities are of the opinion that mince pies were formerly baked in coffin-shaped crusts intended to represent the manger, but in all old cookery-books the crust of a pie was styled the coffin.

It is said, by those who should be able to speak with authority, that ghosts never appear on the night of December 24th—25th. This is a fact that Charles Dickens must have overlooked.

Christmas Proverbs, etc.:—

(a) A warm Christmas, a cold Easter.
(b) A green Christmas, a white Easter.

(c) Christmas in snow, Easter in wind.

(d) Christmas wet, empty granary and barrel.

(e) If there is wind on Christmas Day, there will be much fruit the following year.

(f) Snow at Christmas brings a good hay crop next year.

(g) If Christmas falls on a Sunday, there is good luck in store for all of us.

(h) A child that's born on Christmas Day, is fair, and wise, and good, and gay.

(i) Carols out of season, sorrow without reason.

(j) If Christmas Day on Thursday be,
A windy winter ye shall see:
Windy weather in each week,
And hard tempest, strong and thick.
The summer shall be good and dry,
Corn and beasts will multiply.

(k) Light Christmas, light wheatsheaf. ("Light" here refers to the full moon.)

(l) There is a firm belief that to leave Christmas decorations hanging beyond Twelfth-Night is to bring ill-luck to everybody in the house.

HOLY INNOCENTS' DAY.—December 28th was formerly reckoned as the most unlucky day of the whole year, and few had the temerity to begin any work or start any new undertaking then.

HOGMANAY.—In Scotland, the night of December 31st is known as Hogmanay. Then the fire is "rested," and on no account is it allowed to go out on the hearth, nor is the house swept, nor ashes nor water "thrown out," in case all the luck should be swept out. "Dirt bodes luck." It is lucky to give away food or money, to break a drinking glass accidentally, for a girl to see a man from her window on New Year's morning, and the birth of a child brings good luck to the entire family.

OTHER WEATHER PROPHECIES

A blustering night, a fair day.

One fair day in winter is often the mother of a storm.

A snow winter, a rich summer and autumn.

A summer fog is for fair weather.

A foot deep of rain will kill hay and grain. But a foot deep of snow will make all things grow.

A sunshiny shower never lasts an hour.

A late spring is a great blessing.

A wet spring, a dry harvest.

After a wet year, a cold one.

As the days lengthen, so the cold strengthens.

Between twelve and two, you'll see what the day will do.

Cloudy mornings, clear evenings.

Evenings red and mornings grey help the traveller on his way. Evenings grey and mornings red bring down rain upon his head.

A bee was never caught in a shower.

If fowls roll in the sand, rain is at hand.

If hoar frost comes on mornings twain, the third day surely will have rain.

If Friday be clear, have for Sunday no fear.

If the cock goes crowing to bed, he'll certainly rise with a watery head.

If the moon changes on a Sunday, there will be a flood before the month is out.

If the oak is out before the ash, 'twill be a summer of wet and splash.

If the wind is north-east three days without rain, eight days will pass before south wind again.

Neither give credit to a clear winter nor a cloudy spring.

On Thursday at three, look out and you'll see what Friday will be.

Rain at seven, fine at eleven. Rain at eight, not fine till eight.

It is not spring until one can put down a foot on a dozen daisies.

Mackerel sky, mackerel sky; never long wet and never long dry.

Thunder in spring, cold will bring.

Sharp horns do threaten windy weather (referring to the points of the moon).

When the squirrel eats nuts on a tree, there'll be weather as warm as warm can be.

When the wind veers against the sun, trust it not, for back 'twill run.

When a cow tries to scratch its ear, it means that a storm is very near.

A CALENDAR FOR LOVERS

The information set out below is derived from star-readings and other heavenly data. It applies only to the average individual. The days of the months refer to the birthdays of those whom the information concerns.

JANUARY

1.—Will make a good partner, though desirous of being the ruler.

2.—Likely to marry late.

3.—Women born on this day often marry men younger than themselves.

4.—Will make an excellent partner if allowed to lead a peaceful life.

5.—Likely to marry late, but the union will bring considerable happiness.

6.—Married life will be a success if both partners are prepared to run the home on business lines.

7.—Will be cautious in entering the matrimonial state.

8.—Married life will become more and more a boon, as the years pass by.

9.—Will marry late and have much difficulty in making up his or her mind.

10.—Money matters will cause the greatest concern during married life.

11.—Such an individual will make a difficult partner unless he or she marries someone with a stronger will.

12.—Somewhat slow in deciding on marriage.

13.—Likely to miss rare opportunities by wavering.

14.—Will be critical regarding his or her partner.

15.—A faithful lover, but should avoid too close a relationship with his or her partner's relatives.

16.—Will need a good deal of persuasion or assistance in agreeing to marriage; but will not regret having taken the step, afterwards.

17.—Unduly shy in facing the routine of his or her wedding.

18.—Will want to keep dark the facts of his or her wedding, but not because he or she is ashamed of the partner.

19.—A late marriage.

173

20.—Not likely to show the extent of his or her affections.

21.—Will think overmuch of gaining security in the world before plunging into marriage.

22.—Will probably have an exalted opinion of his or her partner, due to great affection.

23.—A faithful lover.

24.—Likely to marry late and will want to rule the roost.

25.—Slow at expressing feelings of love, but once the mind is made up there will be no wavering.

26.—Such an individual should see that he or she is not marrying on insufficient money. Considerable difficulties are likely to result, if this warning is overlooked.

27.—There will be more love expressed after marriage than before.

28.—Such an individual must seriously question himself or herself whether he or she is really marrying for love.

29.—Not a person to fall in love at first sight.

30.—Love is likely to be a matter of business.

31.—A very faithful lover and one that will take his or her obligations very seriously.

FEBRUARY

1.—Unlikely to marry before a number of romances have been experienced.

2.—Will think worlds of the one he or she marries.

3.—Is not likely to enter matrimony without considering all the "pros and cons."

4.—Likely to put too much faith in his or her partner and to think too highly of him or her.

5.—A rather late marriage, but it will be a real love match when it is eventually planned.

6.—Very likely to consider him or herself unequal to the partner; perhaps unworthy is the more correct description. This erroneous idea should be banished.

7.—Rather slow in showing affection.

8.—It is highly important that this individual marries the right person; otherwise he or she will never be thoroughly happy.

9.—It is "fifty-fifty" whether he or she marries at all.

10.—Probably a breaker of hearts.

11.—Likely to expect the partner to be a paragon of virtue and to be disappointed if he or she is not.

12.—If relations can be kept from interfering, marriage will bring great blessings.

13.—Not likely to marry the person everybody supposes will be the one.

14.—Will make a very kind and attentive partner, if the partner plays a similar role.

15.—Too fond of comforts and one's own company to embark on marriage lightly.

16.—Will expect a great deal from married life. May easily be disappointed.

17.—Will find it difficult to choose the right partner from a large circle of acquaintances.

18.—Marriage will be late.

19.—Will fall in love many times before making the all-important choice.

20.—Will not fall into love unconsciously. It will need an effort.

21.—Nobody will know what this individual thinks in regard to love matters. Most likely he will announce, one day, to the astonishment of all that he is to be married shortly.

22.—A long courtship awaits this person.

23.—Should marry someone with totally different qualities and an entirely different outlook on life.

24.—Will grow to think so highly of his or her partner that life without this person, even for a day, becomes unbearable.

25.—Likely to be fickle.

26.—Men born on this date are liable to find that the girl has formed an attachment elsewhere, while they were weighing up her good qualities. Girls may hesitate to say "yes" and find that the opportunity has passed.

27.—Marriage might easily prove somewhat disappointing.

28.—Such individuals should make absolutely sure of their minds before sealing the bargain.

29.—People born on the twenty-ninth are always considered to be very lucky in matters of love and marriage.

MARCH

1.—There are signs that point to dangerous flirtations.

2.—Greatest happiness will come after the first few years of married life have passed away.

3.—Marriage will mean considerable happiness.

4.—Such individuals have a most compelling way with the opposite sex and they make excellent partners.

5.—Is not likely to remain satisfied with the love of one person.

6.—Marriage for such as you is necessary. It will be the making of you.

7.—A very faithful lover.

8.—Will be extremely happy, if he or she does not rush into marriage and choose the wrong partner.

9.—It is probable that you will have numerous tempting chances to marry. The proper selection will be a matter fraught with great difficulties.

10.—Will treat matrimony too much as a business.

11.—Likely to make a very suitable match.

12.—An early marriage, most likely, not with the person most friends think probable.

13.—A happy married life is almost certain.

14.—This individual will be at his or her wits' ends to make the final and proper decision.

15.—After marriage, this person will thank his or her lucky stars that events have shaped as they have, especially in view of doubt experienced at the moment of deciding.

16.—"A dark horse." Nobody understands him or her, not even the partner for life. This only adds to the individual's attractions.

17.—If this individual works hard, as the horoscope says he or she should, married life will prove a great blessing.

18.—Married life will not be supremely romantic, but it will be congenial.

19.—There are dark patches in this individual's married life. They may be quarrels and estrangements, but they will not be continuous.

20.—He or she will be very faithful and have an extremely high opinion of the partner.

21.—This individual will have unnecessary disappointments, largely through a temperament which blinds him or her to the partner's point of view.

22.—Likely to put up with difficulties rather than cause unpleasantness. Is worthy of better treatment.

23.—The opposite of March 22nd. Is likely to cause trouble for things that hardly matter.

24.—Rather fickle in love affairs.

25.—A very passionate individual. Will only be satisfied with marriage if the partner gives way to him or her on almost all matters.

26.—Very fond of the opposite sex. May find the situation becomes awkward.

27.—A thoughtful individual who will make the partner of the marriage very happy.

28.—Will make a good husband or wife, but money matters may cause difficulties.

29.—This individual may easily take offence at things done by the partner. Otherwise, he or she will be affectionate.

30.—This person will probably show more affection before marriage than after.

31.—A person who will make a charming partner if the one he or she marries sets out to pander to his or her foibles.

APRIL

1.—An early marriage is probable and it should be a very happy one.

2.—Will make a marriage in which the man plays a subordinate part.

3.—The general course of marriage will be very happy, but there are likely to be times of estrangement.

4.—A somewhat rebellious nature is likely to cause occasional difficulties.

5.—Likely to marry without giving the matter all the consideration it deserves.

6.—This individual will probably hesitate before accepting a partner for so long that the opportunity will be missed.

7.—This individual will only be happy in the married state if the partner is particularly amenable.

8.—A rather passionate lover, but the ardor will considerably lessen as time rolls on.

9.—Married life may fall short of expectations because the individual refuses to face difficulties.

10.—Marriage should be undertaken early.

11.—Has great attractions for the opposite sex and is likely to be fickle.

12.—Very affectionate but is likely to overlook the desires of his or her partner.

13.—This individual may neglect his or her partner through being un-thoughtful.

14.—An individual who will be quite content to sail through married life in a placid manner.

15.—Likely to fall in love at first sight.

16.—Will find married life very congenial if he or she takes the upper hand.

17.—An individual who will be difficult to understand, but with better qualities than are usually attributed to him or her.

18.—Will only be happy in married life if the home is artistically planned.

19.—A happy married life if the partner can understand this individual's temperament.

20.—Will marry early.

21.—Love and marriage will be the means of providing considerable happiness.

22.—An individual who will love deeply, but may be inclined to jealousy.

23.—Marriage will be planned and carried out in a very short space of time.

24.—Should avoid marriage with a person of strong likes and dislikes.

25.—The course of true love never runs smoothly, and it will not with this individual.

26.—Warm-hearted, this person will make an admirable partner.

27.—An individual who should not rush into marriage lightly. He or she is liable to be guided more by the heart than the head.

28.—Will make an admirable lover and partner in marriage.

29.—Very emotional, this individual should guard against marrying some-one who is too matter of fact.

30.—An individual who will put the home before everything else.

MAY

1.—A very affectionate person where the right partner is concerned.

2.—Will be most concerned in providing joys for his or her partner.

3.—Is likely to be an admirable husband or wife as long as he or she may indulge in harmless flirtations.

4.—Early married life may have its ups and downs owing to misunderstandings. Later on, things will materially improve, due to a better knowledge of each other.

5.—Very affectionate if allowed to idolize his or her partner.

6.—A very charming lover.

7.—This individual is apt to be swayed by extremes, but on the whole he or she will prove an excellent partner in marriage.

8.—He or she is much too practical to allow petty worries to mar the married life.

9.—An individual who will take marriage very seriously.

10.—Marriage will mean some sacrifices but many joys. It will be tremendously worth while.

11.—An individual who will have numerous "affairs" before settling down to the right partner.

12.—There are disappointments for this partner, and the greatest joys of marriage will only come in middle life.

13.—A person who will expect his or her partner to be perfect. Given this, he or she will be adorable.

14.—Love will be life to this person.

15.—A person who will work hard to give the partner a glorious time.

16.—An individual who will be sought after by numerous members of the opposite sex.

17.—One who will love very deeply.

18.—An individual who will play with love for a long time before giving it serious consideration.

19.—Having a warm heart and a generous nature, this person is sure to bring his partner much happiness.

20.—This individual will have so many attachments that he or she will find difficulty in making the right choice.

21.—An excellent and faithful husband or wife.

22.—This individual will aspire to marrying beyond his or her station.

23.—This person is likely to seek elsewhere, if refused on the first occasion, be he a man. Thus, the prospective bride should be wary of saying "no" out of caprice.

24.—Of a sensitive nature, this person will be very shy in showing his or her feelings.

25.—Rather apt to grumble about the trifles of married life. Quick to notice faults.

26.—This person is likely to work out the affairs of love much as he or she would attend to a tradesman's account.

27.—A person who would prove a more practical than ardent lover.

28.—Very much admired by the opposite sex, but one who is likely to cool down a great deal after marriage.

29.—One who finds it difficult to be more than three-quarters in love.

30.—A number of minor love affairs will suddenly give place to finding the right partner, followed by a speedy marriage.

31.—Likely to be jealous without sufficient cause.

JUNE

1.—An individual who will treat matrimony with a great deal of caution.

2.—Slow in showing affection, but is in earnest when he or she does.

3.—This person will have to be careful if he or she is not to lose the partner, wanted most.

4.—You have a very high opinion of the opposite sex, and your affections are not centered on one person. This will make your married life somewhat difficult.

5.—This person will have difficulty in knowing his or her mind.

6.—Marriage will be the beginning of much happiness.

7.—Do not be discouraged if things appear black at first. The end is what matters most, and things will work out happily.

8.—His or her love affairs must be carefully handled if success is to come of them.

9.—A happy married life is in store.

10.—It will require much tact if the good ship "Matrimony" is to sail the seas of adventure without coming to harm.

11.—This individual may never realize all his or her dreams of matrimony.

12.—Will most likely drift into the married state hardly knowing it.

13.—You are too practical to make anything but a very sensible union.

14.—This individual will have numerous flirtations, then a time of quiet, followed by a happy marriage.

15.—It will require two sensible heads to make a successful marriage.

16.—This individual will look for an accomplished partner who will understand all his or her peculiarities.

17.—Rather given to flirting.

18.—Will not fall into love easily.

19.—This individual will be much esteemed by the opposite sex, more for his or her inner qualities than for those appearing on the surface.

20.—Will make a very charming partner.

21.—This person will make love a matter of fact affair and rob it of its romance.

22.—A person who is apt to delay marriage too long, being afraid of making a mistake.

23.—This person will expect the one he or she marries to be extremely Victorian. There must never be as much as a suspicion of flirting.

24.—He or she will put the home before everything else.

25.—Much liked and even spoiled by the opposite sex, it will be difficult for him or her to settle down comfortably to a married life.

26.—An individual who will never forget the first love.

27.—It is advisable to marry early to avoid entanglements.

28.—A person who will deny him or herself much in order to make his or her partner happy.

29.—Many mistakes before marriage, but a life of great comfort after.

30.—A great decision will have to be made. It will depend on which of two is the better to take.

JULY

1.—This person is likely to choose a partner without taking into consideration all that he or she should.

2.—The course of early love may result in a certain amount of unhappiness.

3.—Likely to marry early, after having experienced several attachments.

4.—There will be more happiness after marriage than before.

5.—This individual will thank his or her lucky stars that someone else was not chosen for a partner. The "someone else" was thought by everybody to be the favorite.

6.—A very attractive lover, but a breaker of hearts.

7.—A married life with several ups and down, but none of them really serious.

8.—This individual belongs to the type of person who marries the girl or man he or she knows best.

9.—Marriage will open a new and more beautiful life for this person.

10.—It is doubtful if this person really wants to marry.

11.—An individual who prefers the excitement of flirtations to the settled life of marriage; that is until it is too late.

12.—Likely to seek a good marriage financially.

13.—A very happy marriage, if interfering relations can be kept at a distance.

14.—Marriage may not be all that is expected of it.

15.—A long courtship followed by a happy union.

16.—Given a partner of worthy character, this individual will bless the day of marriage.

17.—Will think more and more of his or her partner as time wears on.

18.—An individual whose matrimonial affairs will surprise his or her friends.

19.—Many passionate romances will be experienced before the fateful decision is made.

20.—An individual who will wish to be as romantic after the wedding as before.

21.—A very sympathetic lover.

22.—An individual who will show very little affection, but who will have, however, more than his or her share. A peculiarity of temperament will cause him or her to hide it.

23.—Will make an excellent partner.

24.—This individual has only to idolize his or her partner to make a perfect success of married life.

25.—As long as the partner does not wish to rule this person, marriage will be extremely successful.

26.—Great happiness will come of the union as long as both the partners retain their affections for the other.

27.—Many minor love affairs before the right one is experienced.

28.—An individual who is likely to marry someone of a very different age —either considerably older or younger.

29.—A very bright and attractive husband or wife. That is what this individual will be.

30.—A person who will be happy in marriage, as long as finances cause no troubles.

31.—There is little indication that this person troubles much about love matters.

AUGUST

1.—Marriage likely to be rather late.

2.—Will be very generous towards his or her partner.

3.—The first love will never be forgotten by this individual.

4.—The course of true love will not run smoothly at first: later, it will mend.

5.—This person possesses a strong will and, as long as the partner bends to this will, all will be well.

6.—It will be advisable to go slowly. Any undue haste may result in a fiasco.

7.—This individual must put aside all the old loves, once the marriage ceremony has been performed. It will be dangerous to meet them again.

8.—This person will prove a great favorite with the opposite sex. He or she will be so successful that a good deal of caution is needed.

9.—The latter half of the married life will bring the most happiness.

10.—Marriage must be considered from all its angles before the important step is taken: otherwise, disappointments will be caused.

11.—Your generous nature will assure a happy married life.

12.—Several love affairs are indicated before the real one will be experienced. There should be no undue haste in the choosing.

13.—Your happiness in love affairs will not depend so much on you as on those with whom you associate.

14.—Do not become apprehensive if the right partner is slow in coming to you. A rather late marriage is indicated.

15.—There is every reason to think that this individual will choose the right partner and enjoy a happy married life.

16.—It is likely that this person will marry someone well-off.

17.—There is an indication that there may be a break in the engagement, but that the affair will be patched up to the satisfaction of both parties.

18.—Money matters are the only ones that are likely to cause any disagreements in the marriage life. Steer clear of these and all will be well.

19.—Marry before you have settled habits or it will be difficult to make the mutual concessions that marriage entails.

20.—There may be some unhappiness in the early part of your married career.

21.—This person is likely to be very passionate.

22.—Likely to marry late, owing to a desire for personal comforts.

23.—This person will be easily pleased with married life, and the union will be a very happy one if the partner is not of an exacting nature.

24.—Is very fond of the opposite sex. He or she will find some difficulty in deciding whom to marry.

25.—Somewhat fickle. He or she may cause the marriage partner some anxiety on this account.

26.—An individual who will see the utmost good in his or her partner.

27.—This person's marriage will be a proper sequel to the years of courtship.

28.—Married life should bring many joys and blessings.

29.—This person will find it difficult to be satisfied with the love of one person.

30.—This individual will have the power of making his or her partner think worlds of him or her.

31.—A person lacking passion; one who looks upon marriage as a business proposition. The man will marry for a housekeeper; the woman for a roof over her head.

SEPTEMBER

1.—Will make an excellent husband or wife.

2.—Likely to expect too much of marriage.

3.—This individual may tire of marriage if the partner is not decidedly emotional and passionate.

4.—Greatest happiness is likely to come in the middle period of married life. In the early portion, you and your partner will not have learned to understand each other: in the late portion, there will be a tendency for you to go your own ways.

5.—There is a likelihood that secret romances will be continued after the knot has been tied.

6.—You are a little too independent and will not consider the feelings of your partner as much as you should.

7.—There are signs that you may neglect to make love to your partner after the wedding. Then the happiness of both will be jeopardized.

8.—You lack sufficient emotion to make marriage the success it ought to be.

9.—Your marriage may be too much of a business and not enough of a love affair.

10.—You are likely to be drawn to those who are not sufficiently attracted to you. It means that the chances are you will marry late.

11.—Capable of being very affectionate.

12.—Will make an admirable husband or wife. You will be blind to the faults of your partner.

13.—You will fall in love several times and have some difficulty in deciding whom you ought to marry.

14.—A person who is too sensitive in love affairs. Likely to experience some disappointments before marriage.

15.—You are an ardent lover, perhaps too ardent to make the happiest of marriages.

16.—A person likely to enter upon marriage without giving the matter all the consideration it deserves.

17.—Your knowledge of people enables you to judge accurately who will make the best partner to fit in with your ideals.

18.—An individual who has a strong will and who, therefore, can do much towards persuading the person of his or her choice to share life with him or her.

19.—Your love-making will be governed less by your affections than by your reason.

20.—Likely to marry late, as you do not feel your position good enough to share with a partner.

21.—You are likely to be attracted to two very different people at the same time. Your choice ought to be made in favor of the one who more approximates your own station of life.

22.—You can be a delightful companion and ought to make an excellent husband or wife.

23.—Your marriage will make a great difference to you, for the better.

24.—All your love affairs will not bring happiness, but your marriage will be a success.

25.—Probably you will marry a person with whom you fell in love at sight.

26.—Married life will bring considerable happiness, but there will be occasions when your vanity will be hurt and you will then be somewhat morose.

27.—You will usually treat your partner with considerable affection, but there are times when you will speak in a very hasty manner.

28.—You must be careful whom you marry, as you are not likely to be too sure of your own mind.

29.—Likely to have many strings to your bow.

30.—Be very certain that the attachments you form are worthy of you.

OCTOBER

1.—You have a strong desire to create a good impression with the opposite sex. This desire may lead you into danger.

2.—An individual who will make an excellent partner except when he or she is in the wrong. On such occasions he or she will present a very unsympathetic nature.

3.—Marriage will mean everything to such individuals. They must be careful that the wedded state brings no disillusions.

4.—What unhappiness comes in married life will be due to friends who interfere.

5.—Home life will give you the existence you require: therefore you must avoid marriage with a gad-about.

6.—Your marriage will be eminently successful.

7.—You are an individual of somewhat fickle temperament; but you will settle down once you meet the right person.

8.—You are an excellent companion and will make numerous friends of the opposite sex. Choosing the right partner, in your case, will be difficult.

9.—An individual who will love intensely and who has the capacity for making an excellent partner in marriage.

10.—Marriage should be thoroughly successful if financial worries do not upset your calculations.

11.—An individual who will experience much pain as a result of unsuitable friendships.

12.—Likely to find it difficult to remain in love with one person for any length of time.

13.—Married life will bring considerable happiness, but lovemaking should be indulged in after the wedding as much as before.

14.—Your partner will appreciate little surprises, such as tokens of your affection, even after you are married. Do not forget this.

15.—You are liable to be too cold towards your partner. Recall the early days of your friendship.

16.—An individual who will treat married life in a too matter-of-fact way.

17.—Love is not life to you: but once you meet the right person, happiness will reign supreme.

18.—You will approach your love affairs in a very common-sense manner. Thus, you are not likely to make any mistake.

19.—A very worthy partner.

20.—The earlier years of married life will not be the most successful, though they will be the most exciting.

21.—Do not expect every comfort and joy after the wedding ceremony. Money may be a cause of difficulties.

22.—An individual who will experience some trouble in knowing his or her mind.

23.—Slow in acquiring affection; but once a friendship is formed, he or she will be in great earnest.

24.—A happy married life is almost certain.

25.—An individual who is likely to be a more practical than affectionate lover.

26.—Unduly shy in facing the business of a wedding.

27.—This person will have much deeper affections than are suggested by appearances.

28.—Family relations are not likely to make the path of matrimony any rosier.

29.—More love and affection will be expressed after marriage than before.

30.—Rather apt to rule his or her partner when things have settled down after the wedding.

31.—A lover who would satisfy any reasonable being.

NOVEMBER

1.—There will be many surprises for this person.

2.—Great happiness will come of the union, as long as both the partners avoid trouble-making friendships.

3.—Harmless flirtations are hardly harmless, when indulged in by this person.

4.—There will be ups and downs in this person's married life, but the "ups" will exceed the "downs."

5.—This person will not be rebuffed. If a man, he will not take "no" for an answer.

6.—An attractive person with the opposite sex, but likely to cool down a great deal after marriage.

7.—There will be many love affairs, but it is doubtful if marriage will result with any of them.

8.—A person likely to make an admirable partner in marriage, if allowed to follow his or her own harmless way.

9.—Marriage will come early.

10.—A very affectionate lover and marriage partner.

11.—Of a practical nature, this person will know exactly how to steer clear of matrimonial troubles.

12.—Will make an admirable husband or wife.

13.—This person will love very deeply, perhaps too deeply, as it may lead to unfounded jealousy.

14.—It is doubtful if this individual wishes in his heart to marry.

15.—Somewhat fickle in love affairs.

16.—Married life will be less romantic than anticipated, but it will be more congenial and placid.

17.—Too fond of comforts and one's own company to embark on marriage lightly.

18.—This person will be conscious of the fact that he or she invariably falls in love with the wrong person. This will last until the age of 22 or 23 is reached.

19.—Marriage should turn out very well.

20.—A late and happy marriage is indicated.

21.—Likely to be very passionate.

22.—A person who is sure to have several love affairs. A feature of these is that some of them will be revivals of old ones.

23.—Marriage means everything to 'you and you are decidedly unsuited to living a lonely life.

24.—You are sentimental and emotional and will think highly of your partner.

25.—Do not rush into marriage without considering the matter very seriously.

26.—You have an ideal for whom you are searching. However, the ideal does not exist. There are plenty of good fish in the sea, nevertheless.

27.—A rather sudden wedding.

28.—You will be happy only as long as your partner gives you the upper hand.

29.—Marriage will be mixed. Much happiness, some sorrows.

30.—This person will have many love affairs, in fact he or she is the type that prefers a succession of such affairs to settling down to marriage.

DECEMBER

1.—Somewhat headstrong, this person will want to rule the home.

2.—A very easygoing partner. Happy as long as his or her mate guides the ship through the troubled seas.

3.—Men born on this day often marry women older than themselves.

4.—Somewhat slow in deciding on marriage.

5.—Likely to find marriage more of a boon than anticipated.

6.—This person will, probably, marry someone whom nobody anticipated would be the individual.

7.—This individual should marry someone with totally different qualities and an entirely different outlook on life.

8.—Such people have a most compelling way with the opposite sex and they make good partners.

9.—Very fond of the opposite sex; a character that may easily experience difficulties.

10.—Will make a marriage in which the man plays the minor part.

11.—Marriage will be planned and carried out in a short space of time. The haste may be deplored later on.

12.—A person who will take marriage very seriously.

13.—This individual will play at lovemaking for a long time before treating it seriously.

14.—A person who will have numerous flirtations, then a period in which the other sex is more or less ignored, followed by a sudden and happy marriage.

15.—Liable to delay marriage too long, or until it cannot provide the blessings anticipated of it.

16.—Married life will bring many joys and blessings.

17.—Do not be cold and uncommunicative to your partner. Act as you did before the wedding.

18.—You will be slow in acquiring affection. Once a friendship is formed, however, it will be a very deep one.

19.—As long as your partner is not one given to "laying down the law," you will have a very happy existence.

20.—Be very careful that you do not fall in love with someone after marriage.

21.—Marriage will be supremely happy.

22.—You are somewhat fickle and will, probably, suffer in consequence.

23.—Your marriage is likely to have the effect of complicating your financial position.

24.—A person who will find married life of average happiness.

25.—Do not keep from your partner information that should rightly be shared. You are not confiding enough and this may very well cause unhappiness.

26.—Avoid extravagance in married life and all will be well.

27.—A kind and generous partner.

28.—Take little notice of what your friends tell you of your intended one. Be guided by your feelings alone.

29.—You will marry late and your only regret will be that you did not find your partner earlier.

30.—You and your partner will, largely, keep yourselves to yourselves. You will be all in all to each other, and it will prove a very happy existence.

31.—You will make an admirable husband or wife, especially if your partner is one of the "easy-going" type.

MAKING USEFUL MASCOTS

Anyone of a handy disposition can make mascots that will bring luck to him or herself, as well as to countless friends. In addition, they may be made for selling at bazaars or even for profit in shops.

HORSESHOES.—As a rule, it is best in this case to obtain a supply of old and worn horseshoes—any local farrier will be glad to sell them for a penny or two apiece—and to make them presentable. First, knock off the rust, and then wash them if necessary. It is not a bad plan to beg some old nails from the farrier, to slip one or two in the holes, here and there of each shoe, and to twist them round with pliers so that they cannot fall out. Then give the shoes a coat of paint—either aluminum or stove-black. When dry, thread a strip of ribbon of your lucky color through a hole on either side of the shoe, so that the shoe can be easily hung up. But, please do be careful to arrange the ribbon so that the shoe can only be hung tips upwards.

Failing a supply of worn shoes, the best idea is to cut horseshoes from a sheet of thick cardboard. There is an illustration on p. 6 which will give you an idea of the correct shape to aim at. When the shoes are cut, paint them with black or silver ink, and tie with ribbon, as already suggested.

SWASTIKAS.—Large swastikas are best cut out of thick cardboard, as suggested in the previous paragraph for horseshoes, but small ones, suitable for wearing, are not difficult to cut out of sheet metal, if a triangular file is at hand for cleaning up the corners and edges. When worn, Swastikas are usually hung diamond-wise. Therefore, it is necessary to drill a small hole in one of the corners of the shape. A coat of gold paint or transparent lacquer will add to the appearance of the finish.

SCARABS.—When scarabs are to be made, the shape with the closed wings will be found much the simpler to construct. They can be made out of large oval buttons. If the buttons are flat, it is advisable to give them a domed surface by applying a suitable layer of plastic wood. This is a putty-like substance which dries rapidly and which can be moulded to the required shape with the fingers. When the plastic wood is dry and hard, smooth the surface with fine glass-paper and ornament it with oil paints. A dull light blue serves best for the groundwork, and the pattern can be added with a small brush, using grey or black paint. In this way, some very realistic scarabs can be made easily.

CADUCEUS OR STAFF OF MERCURY.—This lucky device is very difficult to make in the form of a model. However, the same purpose can be served by a picture. Draw the outline in pencil (see p. 9), give it a wash of silver color and line in the pattern with India ink. A picture, made in this way, about twelve inches high, on a white card, would look very attractive when framed.

ARROWHEADS.—Those of us who have an eye for geology will have no difficulty in picking up flints, shaped like arrowheads (see p. 8), along the sides of country roads. Failing these, we can get some slips of granite, and, with hammer and chisel, shape them as shown on the page mentioned. The next thing is to obtain some gilt wire, and to make slings to support the arrowheads. These can then be hung up or worn, according to their size.

TETS.—These mallet-shaped mascots can be made readily by cutting small strips of wood to serve as handles, and then moulding the heads in plastic wood. When the latter has dried hard, all the surfaces are coated with some bright colored paint, and, after that, additional bands of color are added to serve as ornamentation (see p. 8).

BLACK CATS AND OTHER DOLL MASCOTS.—Any woman or girl who is good at needlework can make cats and doll-shaped mascots fairly readily. The first thing is to cut a paper pattern of the parts, using newspaper for the purpose. Usually, it is advisable to make the pattern in no more than two parts; one for the left side, the other for the right, or one for the front, the other for the back, according to the way the creature is to be executed. If this is done, it must be recognized that each part should be considerably larger than the animal is to appear, since although the pattern looks as though it need only serve for the front or back, or sides, it really has to supply the width as well.

When the paper pattern has been suitably shaped, cut out the stuff to agree with it, allowing an edging for turning in. Use black velvet or black fur cloth, unless some color is desired. Then, place the two pieces together, face to face, stitch round most of the edges; follow by turning the outside in and stuff the interior through the gap of stitches. Old but soft rags do for the stuffing. When nice and evenly plump, stitch up the gap, taking care to fold in the seams.

The last stage is to ornament the creature and form its features. Buttons serve for eyes, stitches of red wool or silk make the mouth and nose, and whiskers are supplied by hairs taken from a broom. A band of ribbon, tied in a bow, round the neck, completes the mascot.

A CATALOG OF SELECTED DOVER
BOOKS IN ALL FIELDS OF INTEREST

100 BEST-LOVED POEMS, Edited by Philip Smith. *"The Passionate Shepherd to His Love," "Shall I compare thee to a summer's day?" "Death, be not proud," "The Raven," "The Road Not Taken,"* plus works by Blake, Wordsworth, Byron, Shelley, Keats, many others. Includes 13 selections from the Common Core State Standards Initiative. 112pp.   0-486-28553-7

1000 TURN-OF-THE-CENTURY HOUSES: With Illustrations and Floor Plans, Herbert C. Chivers. Reproduced from a rare edition, this showcase of homes ranges from cottages and bungalows to sprawling mansions. Each house is meticulously illustrated and accompanied by complete floor plans. 256pp.   0-486-45596-3

101 GREAT AMERICAN POEMS, Edited by The American Poetry & Literacy Project. Rich treasury of verse from the 19th and 20th centuries includes works by Edgar Allan Poe, Robert Frost, Walt Whitman, Langston Hughes, Emily Dickinson, T. S. Eliot, other notables. Includes 13 selections from the Common Core State Standards Initiative. 96pp.   0-486-40158-8

20TH-CENTURY FASHION ILLUSTRATION: The Feminine Ideal, Rosemary Torre. Introduction by Harold Koda. This captivating retrospective explores the social context of fashion with informative text and over 70 striking images. Profiles include flappers, glamour girls, flower children, and the modern obsession with celebrity styles. 176pp.   0-486-46963-8

3200 OLD-TIME CUTS AND ORNAMENTS, Edited by Blanche Cirker. Royalty-free pictures from 1909 French typography catalog: plants, animals, religious motifs, music, carriages, boats, sports, furniture, clothing; plus borders, banners, wreaths, and other ornaments. Over 3,200 black-and-white illustrations. 112pp.   0-486-41732-8

500 YEARS OF ILLUSTRATION: From Albrecht Dürer to Rockwell Kent, Howard Simon. Unrivaled treasury of art from the 1500s through the 1900s includes drawings by Goya, Hogarth, Dürer, Morris, Doré, Beardsley, others. Hundreds of illustrations, brief introductions. Ideal as reference and browsing book. 512pp.   0-486-48465-3

ABC BOOK OF EARLY AMERICANA, Eric Sloane. Artist and historian Eric Sloane presents a wondrous A-to-Z collection of American innovations, including hex signs, ear trumpets, popcorn, and rocking chairs. Illustrated, hand-lettered pages feature brief captions explaining objects' origins and uses. 64pp.   0-486-49808-5

ADVENTURES OF HUCKLEBERRY FINN, Mark Twain. Join Huck and Jim as their boyhood adventures along the Mississippi River lead them into a world of excitement, danger, and self-discovery. Humorous narrative, lyrical descriptions of the Mississippi valley, and memorable characters. 224pp.   0-486-28061-6

ALICE STARMORE'S BOOK OF FAIR ISLE KNITTING, Alice Starmore. A noted designer from the region of Scotland's Fair Isle explores the history and techniques of this distinctive, stranded-color knitting style and provides copious illustrated instructions for 14 original knitwear designs. 208pp.   0-486-47218-3

ALICE'S ADVENTURES IN WONDERLAND, Lewis Carroll. Beloved classic about a little girl lost in a topsy-turvy land and her encounters with the White Rabbit, March Hare, Mad Hatter, Cheshire Cat, and other delightfully improbable characters. 42 illustrations by Sir John Tenniel. A selection of the Common Core State Standards Initiative. 96pp. 0-486-27543-4

AMERICAN BALLADS AND FOLK SONGS, John A. Lomax and Alan Lomax. Music and lyrics for over 200 songs. *John Henry, Goin' Home, Little Brown Jug, Alabama-Bound, Black Betty, The Hammer Song, Jesse James, Down in the Valley, The Ballad of Davy Crockett,* and many more. 672pp. 0-486-28276-7

AMERICAN LOCOMOTIVES IN HISTORIC PHOTOGRAPHS: 1858 to 1949, Ron Ziel. A rare collection of 126 meticulously detailed official photographs, called "builder portraits," majestically chronicle the rise of steam locomotive power in America. Introduction. Detailed captions. 140pp. 0-486-27393-8

ANIMALS: 1,419 Copyright-Free Illustrations of Mammals, Birds, Fish, Insects, etc, Selected by Jim Harter. Selected for its visual impact and ease of use, this outstanding collection of wood engravings presents over 1,000 species of animals in extremely lifelike poses. Includes mammals, birds, reptiles, amphibians, fish, insects, and other invertebrates. 284pp. 0-486-23766-4

THE ANNOTATED INNOCENCE OF FATHER BROWN, G. K. Chesterton. Twelve of the popular Father Brown mysteries appear in this copiously annotated edition. Includes "The Blue Cross," "The Hammer of God," "The Eye of Apollo," and more. 352pp. 0-486-29859-0

ANTIGONE, Sophocles. Filled with passionate speeches and sensitive probing of moral and philosophical issues, this powerful and often-performed Greek drama reveals the grim fate that befalls the children of Oedipus. Footnotes. 64pp. 0-486-27804-2

ART FORMS IN NATURE, Ernst Haeckel. Multitude of strangely beautiful natural forms: Radiolaria, Foraminifera, Ciliata, diatoms, calcareous sponges, Tubulariidae, Siphonophora, Semaeostomeae, star corals, starfishes, much more. All images in black and white. 100pp. 0-486-22987-4

THE ART OF WAR, Sun Tzu. Widely regarded as "The Oldest Military Treatise in the World," this landmark work covers principles of strategy, tactics, maneuvering, communication, and supplies; the use of terrain, fire, and the seasons of the year; much more. 96pp. 0-486-42557-6

THE ARTHUR RACKHAM TREASURY: 86 Full-Color Illustrations, Arthur Rackham. Selected and Edited by Jeff A. Menges. A stunning treasury of 86 full-page plates span the famed English artist's career, from *Rip Van Winkle* (1905) to masterworks such as *Undine, A Midsummer Night's Dream,* and *Wind in the Willows* (1939). 96pp. 0-486-44685-9

THE AUTHENTIC GILBERT & SULLIVAN SONGBOOK, W. S. Gilbert and A. S. Sullivan. The most comprehensive collection available, this songbook includes selections from every one of Gilbert and Sullivan's light operas. Ninety-two numbers are presented uncut and unedited, and in their original keys. 410pp. 0-486-23482-7

THE AUTOCRAT OF THE BREAKFAST-TABLE, Oliver Wendell Holmes. Witty, easy-to-read philosophical essays, written by the poet, essayist, and professor. Holmes drew upon his experiences as a resident of a New England boardinghouse to add color and humor to these reflections. 240pp. 0-486-79028-2

THE AWAKENING, Kate Chopin. First published in 1899, this controversial novel of a New Orleans wife's search for love outside a stifling marriage shocked readers. Today, it remains a first-rate narrative with superb characterization. New introductory note. 128pp. 0-486-27786-0

BASEBALL IS . . .: Defining the National Pastime, Edited by Paul Dickson. Wisecracking, philosophical, nostalgic, and entertaining, these hundreds of quips and observations by players, their wives, managers, authors, and others cover every aspect of our national pastime. It's a great any-occasion gift for fans! 256pp. 0-486-48209-X

BEETHOVEN'S LETTERS, Ludwig van Beethoven. Edited by Dr. A. C. Kalischer. Features 457 letters to fellow musicians, friends, greats, patrons, and literary men. Reveals musical thoughts, quirks of personality, insights, and daily events. Includes 15 plates. 410pp. 0-486-22769-3

BOUND & DETERMINED: A Visual History of Corsets, 1850–1960, Kristina Seleshanko. This revealing history of corsetry ranges from the 19th through the mid-20th centuries to show how simple laced bodices developed into corsets of cane, whalebone, and steel. Lavish illustrations include line drawings and photographs. 128pp. 0-486-47892-0

THE BUILDING OF MANHATTAN, Written and Illustrated by Donald A. Mackay. Meticulously accurate line drawings and fascinating text explain construction above and below ground, including excavating subway lines and building bridges and skyscrapers. Hundreds of illustrations reveal intricate details of construction techniques. A selection of the Common Core State Standards Initiative. 160pp. 0-486-47317-1

THE BUNGALOW BOOK: Floor Plans and Photos of 112 Houses, 1910, Henry L. Wilson. Here are 112 of the most popular and economic blueprints of the early 20th century — plus an illustration or photograph of each completed house. A wonderful time capsule that still offers a wealth of valuable insights. 160pp. 0-486-45104-6

THE CALL OF THE WILD, Jack London. A classic novel of adventure, drawn from London's own experiences as a Klondike adventurer, relating the story of a heroic dog caught in the brutal life of the Alaska Gold Rush. Note. 64pp. 0-486-26472-6

CANDIDE, Voltaire. Edited by Francois-Marie Arouet. One of the world's great satires since its first publication in 1759. Witty, caustic skewering of romance, science, philosophy, religion, government — nearly all human ideals and institutions. A selection of the Common Core State Standards Initiative. 112pp. 0-486-26689-3

THE CARTOON HISTORY OF TIME, Kate Charlesworth and John Gribbin. Cartoon characters explain cosmology, quantum physics, and other concepts covered by Stephen Hawking's *A Brief History of Time*. Humorous graphic novel–style treatment, perfect for young readers and curious folk of all ages. 64pp. 0-486-49097-1

THE CHERRY ORCHARD, Anton Chekhov. Classic of world drama concerns passing of semifeudal order in turn-of-the-century Russia, symbolized in the sale of the cherry orchard owned by Madame Ranevskaya. Showcases Chekhov's rich sensitivities as an observer of human nature. 64pp. 0-486-26682-6

A CHRISTMAS CAROL, Charles Dickens. This engrossing tale relates Ebenezer Scrooge's ghostly journeys through Christmases past, present, and future and his ultimate transformation from a harsh and grasping old miser to a charitable and compassionate human being. 80pp. 0-486-26865-9

COMMON SENSE, Thomas Paine. First published in January of 1776, this highly influential landmark document clearly and persuasively argued for American separation from Great Britain and paved the way for the Declaration of Independence. A selection of the Common Core State Standards Initiative. 64pp. 0-486-29602-4

THE COMPLETE SHORT STORIES OF OSCAR WILDE, Oscar Wilde. Complete texts of "The Happy Prince and Other Tales," "A House of Pomegranates," "Lord Arthur Savile's Crime and Other Stories," "Poems in Prose," and "The Portrait of Mr. W. H." 208pp. 0-486-45216-6

COMPLETE SONNETS, William Shakespeare. Over 150 exquisite poems deal with love, friendship, the tyranny of time, beauty's evanescence, death, and other themes in language of remarkable power, precision, and beauty. Glossary of archaic terms. Includes a selection from the Common Core State Standards Initiative. 80pp. 0-486-26686-9

THE COUNT OF MONTE CRISTO: Abridged Edition, Alexandre Dumas. Falsely accused of treason, Edmond Dantès is imprisoned in the bleak Chateau d'If. After a hair-raising escape, he launches an elaborate plot to extract a bitter revenge against those who betrayed him. 448pp. 0-486-45643-9

CRAFTSMAN BUNGALOWS: 59 Homes from "The Craftsman," Edited by Gustav Stickley. Best and most attractive designs from the Arts and Crafts Movement publication from 1903 to 1916 includes sketches, photographs of homes, floor plans, and descriptive text. 128pp. 0-486-25829-7

CRIME AND PUNISHMENT, Fyodor Dostoyevsky. Translated by Constance Garnett. Supreme masterpiece tells the story of Raskolnikov, a student tormented by his own thoughts after he murders an old woman. Overwhelmed by guilt and terror, he confesses and goes to prison. A selection of the Common Core State Standards Initiative. 448pp. 0-486-41587-2

CYRANO DE BERGERAC, Edmond Rostand. A quarrelsome, hot-tempered, and unattractive swordsman falls hopelessly in love with a beautiful woman and woos her for a handsome but slow-witted suitor. A witty and eloquent drama. 144pp. 0-486-41119-2

DANIEL BOONE'S OWN STORY & THE ADVENTURES OF DANIEL BOONE, Daniel Boone and Francis Lister Hawks. This two-part tale features reminiscences in the legendary frontiersman's own words and a profile of his entire life, with exciting accounts of blazing the Wilderness Road and serving as a militiaman during the Revolutionary War. 128pp. 0-486-47690-1

THE DECLARATION OF INDEPENDENCE AND OTHER GREAT DOCUMENTS OF AMERICAN HISTORY: 1775-1865, Edited by John Grafton. Thirteen compelling and influential documents: Henry's "Give Me Liberty or Give Me Death," Declaration of Independence, The Constitution, Washington's First Inaugural Address, The Monroe Doctrine, The Emancipation Proclamation, Gettysburg Address, more. Includes 3 selections from the Common Core State Standards Initiative. 64pp. 0-486-41124-9

A DOLL'S HOUSE, Henrik Ibsen. Ibsen's best-known play displays his genius for realistic prose drama. An expression of women's rights, the play climaxes when the central character, Nora, rejects a smothering marriage and life in "a doll's house." A selection of the Common Core State Standards Initiative. 80pp. 0-486-27062-9

DOOMED SHIPS: Great Ocean Liner Disasters, William H. Miller, Jr. Nearly 200 photographs, many from private collections, highlight tales of some of the vessels whose pleasure cruises ended in catastrophe: the *Morro Castle*, *Normandie*, *Andrea Doria*, *Europa*, and many others. 128pp. 0-486-45366-9

THE DORÉ BIBLE ILLUSTRATIONS, Gustave Doré. Detailed plates from the Bible: the Creation scenes, Adam and Eve, horrifying visions of the Flood, the battle sequences with their monumental crowds, depictions of the life of Jesus, 241 plates in all. 241pp. 0-486-23004-X

DUBLINERS, James Joyce. A fine and accessible introduction to the work of one of the 20th century's most influential writers, this collection features 15 tales, including a masterpiece of the short-story genre, "The Dead." 160pp. 0-486-26870-5

THE EARLY SCIENCE FICTION OF PHILIP K. DICK, Philip K. Dick. This anthology presents short stories and novellas that originally appeared in pulp magazines of the early 1950s, including "The Variable Man," "Second Variety," "Beyond the Door," "The Defenders," and more. 272pp. 0-486-49733-X

Browse over 10,000 books at www.doverpublications.com

THE EARLY SHORT STORIES OF F. SCOTT FITZGERALD, F. Scott Fitzgerald. These tales offer insights into many themes, characters, and techniques that emerged in Fitzgerald's later works. Selections include "The Curious Case of Benjamin Button," "Babes in the Woods," and a dozen others. 256pp. 0-486-79465-2

EASY BUTTERFLY ORIGAMI, Tammy Yee. Thirty full-color designs to fold include simple instructions and fun facts about each species. Patterns are perforated for easy removal and offer accurate portrayals of variations in insects' top and bottom sides. 64pp. 0-486-78457-6

EASY SPANISH PHRASE BOOK NEW EDITION: Over 700 Phrases for Everyday Use, Pablo Garcia Loaeza, Ph.D. Up-to-date volume, organized for quick access to phrases related to greetings, transportation, shopping, emergencies, other common circumstances. Over 700 entries include terms for modern telecommunications, idioms, slang. Phonetic pronunciations accompany phrases. 96pp. 0-486-49905-7

EINSTEIN'S ESSAYS IN SCIENCE, Albert Einstein. Speeches and essays in accessible, everyday language profile influential physicists such as Niels Bohr and Isaac Newton. They also explore areas of physics to which the author made major contributions. 128pp. 0-486-47011-3

EL DORADO: Further Adventures of the Scarlet Pimpernel, Baroness Orczy. A popular sequel to *The Scarlet Pimpernel*, this suspenseful story recounts the Pimpernel's attempts to rescue the Dauphin from imprisonment during the French Revolution. An irresistible blend of intrigue, period detail, and vibrant characterizations. 352pp. 0-486-44026-5

ELEGANT SMALL HOMES OF THE TWENTIES: 99 Designs from a Competition, Chicago Tribune. Nearly 100 designs for five- and six-room houses feature New England and Southern colonials, Normandy cottages, stately Italianate dwellings, and other fascinating snapshots of American domestic architecture of the 1920s. 112pp. 0-486-46910-7

THE ELUSIVE PIMPERNEL, Baroness Orczy. Robespierre's revolutionaries find their wicked schemes thwarted by the heroic Pimpernel — Sir Percival Blakeney. In this thrilling sequel, Chauvelin devises a plot to eliminate the Pimpernel and his wife. 272pp. 0-486-45464-9

ERIC SLOANE'S WEATHER BOOK, Eric Sloane. A beautifully illustrated book of enlightening lore for outdoorsmen, farmers, sailors, and anyone who has ever wondered whether to take an umbrella when leaving the house. 87 illustrations. 96pp. 0-486-44357-4

ETHAN FROME, Edith Wharton. Classic story of wasted lives, set against a bleak New England background. Superbly delineated characters in a hauntingly grim tale of thwarted love. Considered by many to be Wharton's masterpiece. 96pp. 0-486-26690-7

THE FEDERALIST PAPERS, Alexander Hamilton, James Madison, John Jay. A collection of 85 articles and essays that were initially published anonymously in New York newspapers in 1787–1788, this volume reflects the intentions of the Constitution's framers and ratifiers. 448pp. 0-486-49636-8

FINDING YOUR WAY WITHOUT MAP OR COMPASS, Harold Gatty. Useful, instructive manual shows would-be explorers, hikers, bikers, scouts, sailors, and survivalists how to find their way outdoors by observing animals, weather patterns, shifting sands, and other elements of nature. 288pp. 0-486-40613-X

FIRST SPANISH READER: A Beginner's Dual-Language Book, Edited by Angel Flores. Delightful stories, other material based on works of Don Juan Manuel, Luis Taboada, Ricardo Palma, other noted writers. Complete faithful English translations on facing pages. Exercises. 176pp. 0-486-25810-6

FIVE ACRES AND INDEPENDENCE, M. G. Kains. This classic of the back-to-the-land movement is packed with solid, timeless information. Written by a renowned horticulturist, it has taught generations how to make their land self-sufficient. 95 figures. 397pp. 0-486-20974-1

FLATLAND: A Romance of Many Dimensions, Edwin A. Abbott. Classic of science (and mathematical) fiction — charmingly illustrated by the author — describes the adventures of A. Square, a resident of Flatland, in Spaceland (three dimensions), Lineland (one dimension), and Pointland (no dimensions). 96pp. 0-486-27263-X

FRANKENSTEIN, Mary Shelley. The story of Victor Frankenstein's monstrous creation and the havoc it caused has enthralled generations of readers and inspired countless writers of horror and suspense. With the author's own 1831 introduction. 176pp. 0-486-28211-2

THE GARGOYLE BOOK: 572 Examples from Gothic Architecture, Lester Burbank Bridaham. Dispelling the conventional wisdom that French Gothic architectural flourishes were born of despair or gloom, Bridaham reveals the whimsical nature of these creations and the ingenious artisans who made them. 572 illustrations. 224pp. 0-486-44754-5

THE GIFT OF THE MAGI AND OTHER SHORT STORIES, O. Henry. Sixteen captivating stories by one of America's most popular storytellers. Included are such classics as "The Gift of the Magi," "The Last Leaf," and "The Ransom of Red Chief." Publisher's Note. A selection of the Common Core State Standards Initiative. 96pp. 0-486-27061-0

THE GÖDELIAN PUZZLE BOOK: Puzzles, Paradoxes and Proofs, Raymond M. Smullyan. These logic puzzles provide entertaining variations on Gödel's incompleteness theorems, offering ingenious challenges related to infinity, truth and provability, undecidability, and other concepts. No background in formal logic is necessary. 288pp. 0-486-49705-4

THE GOETHE TREASURY: Selected Prose and Poetry, Johann Wolfgang von Goethe. Edited, Selected, and with an Introduction by Thomas Mann. In addition to his lyric poetry, Goethe wrote travel sketches, autobiographical studies, essays, letters, and proverbs in rhyme and prose. This collection presents outstanding examples from each genre. 368pp. 0-486-44780-4

GREAT EXPECTATIONS, Charles Dickens. Orphaned Pip is apprenticed to the dirty work of the forge but dreams of becoming a gentleman — and one day finds himself in possession of "great expectations." Dickens' finest novel. 384pp. 0-486-41586-4

GREAT ILLUSTRATIONS BY N. C. WYETH, N. C. Wyeth. Edited and with an Introduction by Jeff A. Menges. This full-color collection focuses on the artist's early and most popular illustrations, featuring more than 100 images from *The Mysterious Stranger, Robin Hood, Robinson Crusoe, The Boy's King Arthur,* and other classics. 128pp. 0-486-47295-7

HAMLET, William Shakespeare. The quintessential Shakespearean tragedy, whose highly charged confrontations and anguished soliloquies probe depths of human feeling rarely sounded in any art. Reprinted from an authoritative British edition complete with illuminating footnotes. A selection of the Common Core State Standards Initiative. 128pp. 0-486-27278-8

THE HAUNTED HOUSE, Charles Dickens. A Yuletide gathering in an eerie country retreat provides the backdrop for Dickens and his friends — including Elizabeth Gaskell and Wilkie Collins — who take turns spinning supernatural yarns. 144pp. 0-486-46309-5

THE HEADS OF CERBERUS, Francis Stevens. Illustrated by Ric Binkley. A trio of time-travelers land in Philadelphia's brutal totalitarian state of 2118. Loaded with action and humor, this 1919 classic was the first alternate-world fantasy. "A much-sought rarity." — *Analog.* 192pp. 0-486-79026-6

HEART OF DARKNESS, Joseph Conrad. Dark allegory of a journey up the Congo River and the narrator's encounter with the mysterious Mr. Kurtz. Masterly blend of adventure, character study, psychological penetration. For many, Conrad's finest, most enigmatic story. 80pp. 0-486-26464-5

HISTORIC COSTUMES AND HOW TO MAKE THEM, Mary Fernald and E. Shenton. Practical, informative guidebook shows how to create everything from short tunics worn by Saxon men in the fifth century to a lady's bustle dress of the late 1800s. 81 illustrations. 176pp. 0-486-44906-8

THE HOUND OF THE BASKERVILLES, Sir Arthur Conan Doyle. A deadly curse in the form of a legendary ferocious beast continues to claim its victims from the Baskerville family until Holmes and Watson intervene. Often called the best detective story ever written. 128pp. 0-486-28214-7

THE HOUSE BEHIND THE CEDARS, Charles W. Chesnutt. Originally published in 1900, this groundbreaking novel by a distinguished African-American author recounts the drama of a brother and sister who "pass for white" during the dangerous days of Reconstruction. 208pp. 0-486-46144-0

HOW THE OTHER HALF LIVES, Jacob Riis. This famous journalistic record of the filth and degradation of New York's slums at the turn of the 20th century is a classic in social thought and of early American photography. Over 100 photographs. 256pp. 0-486-22012-5

HOW TO DRAW NEARLY EVERYTHING, Victor Perard. Beginners of all ages can learn to draw figures, faces, landscapes, trees, flowers, and animals of all kinds. Well-illustrated guide offers suggestions for pencil, pen, and brush techniques plus composition, shading, and perspective. 160pp. 0-486-49848-4

HOW TO MAKE SUPER POP-UPS, Joan Irvine. Illustrated by Linda Hendry. Super pop-ups extend the element of surprise with three-dimensional designs that slide, turn, spring, and snap. More than 30 patterns and 475 illustrations include cards, stage props, and school projects. 96pp. 0-486-46589-6

THE IMITATION OF CHRIST, Thomas à Kempis. Translated by Aloysius Croft and Harold Bolton. This religious classic has brought understanding and comfort to millions for centuries. Written in a candid and conversational style, the topics include liberation from worldly inclinations, preparation and consolations of prayer, and eucharistic communion. 160pp. 0-486-43185-1

THE IMPORTANCE OF BEING EARNEST, Oscar Wilde. Wilde's witty and buoyant comedy of manners, filled with some of literature's most famous epigrams, reprinted from an authoritative British edition. Considered Wilde's most perfect work. A selection of the Common Core State Standards Initiative. 64pp. 0-486-26478-5

THE INFERNO, Dante Alighieri. Translated and with notes by Henry Wadsworth Longfellow. The first stop on Dante's famous journey from Hell to Purgatory to Paradise, this 14th-century allegorical poem blends vivid and shocking imagery with graceful lyricism. Translated by the beloved 19th-century poet, Henry Wadsworth Longfellow. 256pp. 0-486-44288-8

JANE EYRE, Charlotte Brontë. Written in 1847, *Jane Eyre* tells the tale of an orphan girl's progress from the custody of cruel relatives to an oppressive boarding school and its culmination in a troubled career as a governess. A selection of the Common Core State Standards Initiative. 448pp. 0-486-42449-9

JAPANESE WOODBLOCK BIRD PRINTS, Numata Kashû. These lifelike images of birds and flowers first appeared in a now-rare 1883 portfolio. A magnificent reproduction of a 1938 facsimile of the original publication, this exquisite edition features 150 color illustrations. 160pp. 0-486-47050-4

Browse over 10,000 books at www.doverpublications.com

JULIUS CAESAR, William Shakespeare. Great tragedy based on Plutarch's account of the lives of Brutus, Julius Caesar, and Mark Antony. Evil plotting, ringing oratory, high tragedy with Shakespeare's incomparable insight, dramatic power. Explanatory footnotes. 96pp. 0-486-26876-4

THE JUNGLE, Upton Sinclair. 1906 bestseller shockingly reveals intolerable labor practices and working conditions in the Chicago stockyards as it tells the grim story of a Slavic family that emigrates to America full of optimism but soon faces despair. 304pp. 0-486-41923-1

JUST WHAT THE DOCTOR DISORDERED: Early Writings and Cartoons of Dr. Seuss, Dr. Seuss. Edited and with an Introduction by Rick Marschall. The Doctor's visual hilarity, nonsense language, and offbeat sense of humor illuminate this compilation of items from his early career, created for periodicals such as *Judge*, *Life*, *College Humor*, and *Liberty*. 144pp. 0-486-49846-8

KING LEAR, William Shakespeare. Powerful tragedy of an aging king, betrayed by his daughters, robbed of his kingdom, descending into madness. Perhaps the bleakest of Shakespeare's tragic dramas, complete with explanatory footnotes. 144pp. 0-486-28058-6

KNITTING FOR ANARCHISTS: The What, Why and How of Knitting, Anna Zilboorg. Every knitter takes a different approach, and this revolutionary guide encourages experimentation and self-expression. Suitable for active knitters and beginners alike, it offers illustrated patterns for sweaters, pullovers, and cardigans. 160pp. 0-486-79466-0

THE LADY OR THE TIGER?: and Other Logic Puzzles, Raymond M. Smullyan. Created by a renowned puzzle master, these whimsically themed challenges involve paradoxes about probability, time, and change; metapuzzles; and self-referentiality. Nineteen chapters advance in difficulty from relatively simple to highly complex. 1982 edition. 240pp. 0-486-47027-X

LEAVES OF GRASS: The Original 1855 Edition, Walt Whitman. Whitman's immortal collection includes some of the greatest poems of modern times, including his masterpiece, "Song of Myself." Shattering standard conventions, it stands as an unabashed celebration of body and nature. 128pp. 0-486-45676-5

LES MISÉRABLES, Victor Hugo. Translated by Charles E. Wilbour. Abridged by James K. Robinson. A convict's heroic struggle for justice and redemption plays out against a fiery backdrop of the Napoleonic wars. This edition features the excellent original translation and a sensitive abridgment. 304pp. 0-486-45789-3

LIGHT FOR THE ARTIST, Ted Seth Jacobs. Intermediate and advanced art students receive a broad vocabulary of effects with this in-depth study of light. Diagrams and paintings illustrate applications of principles to figure, still life, and landscape paintings. 144pp. 0-486-49304-0

LILITH: A Romance, George MacDonald. In this novel by the father of fantasy literature, a man travels through time to meet Adam and Eve and to explore humanity's fall from grace and ultimate redemption. 240pp. 0-486-46818-6

LINE: An Art Study, Edmund J. Sullivan. Written by a noted artist and teacher, this well-illustrated guide introduces the basics of line drawing. Topics include third and fourth dimensions, formal perspective, shade and shadow, figure drawing, and other essentials. 208pp. 0-486-79484-9

THE LODGER, Marie Belloc Lowndes. Acclaimed by *The New York Times* as "one of the best suspense novels ever written," this novel recounts an English couple's doubts about their boarder, whom they suspect of being a serial killer. 240pp. 0-486-78809-1

"THE LOVELIEST HOME THAT EVER WAS": The Story of the Mark Twain House in Hartford, Steve Courtney. With an Introduction by Hal Holbrook. The official guide to The Mark Twain House & Museum, this volume tells the dramatic story of the author and his family and their Victorian mansion. Architectural drawings, period photos, plus modern color images. 144pp. 0-486-48634-6

MACBETH, William Shakespeare. A Scottish nobleman murders the king in order to succeed to the throne. Tortured by his conscience and fearful of discovery, he becomes tangled in a web of treachery and deceit that ultimately spells his doom. A selection of the Common Core State Standards Initiative. 96pp. 0-486-27802-6

MANHATTAN IN MAPS 1527–2014, Paul E. Cohen and Robert T. Augustyn. This handsome volume features 65 full-color maps charting Manhattan's development from the first Dutch settlement to the present. Each map is placed in context by an accompanying essay. 176pp. 0-486-77991-2

MANHATTAN MOVES UPTOWN: An Illustrated History, Charles Lockwood. Compiled from newspaper archives and richly illustrated with historic images, this fascinating chronicle traces the city's growth from Wall Street to Harlem during the period between 1783 and the early 20th century. 368pp. 0-486-78120-8

MATHEMATICS FOR THE NONMATHEMATICIAN, Morris Kline. Erudite and entertaining overview follows development of mathematics from ancient Greeks to present. Topics include logic and mathematics, the fundamental concept, differential calculus, probability theory, much more. Exercises and problems. 672pp. 0-486-24823-2

MEDEA, Euripides. One of the most powerful and enduring of Greek tragedies, masterfully portraying the fierce motives driving Medea's pursuit of vengeance for her husband's insult and betrayal. Authoritative Rex Warner translation. 64pp. 0-486-27548-5

THE MERCHANT BANKERS, Joseph Wechsberg. With a new Foreword by Christopher Kobrak. Fascinating chronicle of the world's great financial families profiles the personalities behind seven legendary banking houses: Hambros, Barings, the Rothschilds, the Warburgs, Deutsche Bank, Lehman Brothers, and Banca Commerciale Italiana. 384pp. 0-486-78118-6

THE METAMORPHOSIS AND OTHER STORIES, Franz Kafka. Excellent new English translations of title story (considered by many critics Kafka's most perfect work), plus "The Judgment," "In the Penal Colony," "A Country Doctor," and "A Report to an Academy." A selection of the Common Core State Standards Initiative. 96pp. 0-486-29030-1

METROPOLIS, Thea von Harbou. This Weimar-era novel of a futuristic society, written by the screenwriter for the iconic 1927 film, was hailed by noted science-fiction authority Forrest J. Ackerman as "a work of genius." 224pp. 0-486-79567-5

MICHAEL PEARSON'S TRADITIONAL KNITTING: Aran, Fair Isle and Fisher Ganseys, New & Expanded Edition, Michael Pearson. This extensive record of unique patterns from the remote fishing villages of Scotland and England combines a social history of the regions with detailed patterns and practical instructions for knitters. Includes new pattern charts and knitting instructions. 264pp. 0-486-46053-3

A MIDSUMMER NIGHT'S DREAM, William Shakespeare. Among the most popular of Shakespeare's comedies, this enchanting play humorously celebrates the vagaries of love as it focuses upon the intertwined romances of several pairs of lovers. Explanatory footnotes. 80pp. 0-486-27067-X

MODULAR CROCHET: The Revolutionary Method for Creating Custom-Designed Pullovers, Judith Copeland. This guide ranks among the most revolutionary and revered books on freeform and improvisational crochet. Even beginners can use its innovative but simple method to make perfect-fit pullovers, turtlenecks, vests, and other garments. 192pp. 0-486-79687-6

Browse over 10,000 books at www.doverpublications.com